# Teaching About
# Winter Holidays
# With Favorite Picture Books

BY IMMACULA A. RHODES

NEW YORK • TORONTO • LONDON • AUCKLAND • SYDNEY
MEXICO CITY • NEW DELHI • HONG KONG • BUENOS AIRES

SCHOLASTIC
Teaching
Resources

To Grandma,

and in loving memory of Grandpa,

for the gift of so many family-filled

holiday memories.

*"Every good and perfect gift is from above..."*

—JAMES 1:17

Cover from LION DANCER: ERNIE WAN'S CHINESE NEW YEAR by Kate Waters, photographs by Martha Cooper. Photographs © 1990 by Martha Cooper. Reprinted by permission of Scholastic Inc.

Cover from ON HANUKKAH reprinted with permission of Atheneum Books for Young Readers, an imprint of Simon & Schuster Children's Publishing Division from ON HANUKKAH by Cathy Goldberg Fishman, illustrated by Melanie W. Hall. Jacket illustration copyright © 1998 by Melanie W. Hall.

Cover from SANTA WHO? by Gail Gibbons. Copyright © 1999 by Gail Gibbons. Reprinted by permission of HarperCollins Children's Books.

Cover from SEVEN CANDLES FOR KWANZAA by Andrea Davis Pinkney, pictures by Brian Pinkney, copyright © 1993 by Brian Pinkney, pictures. Used by permission of Dial Books for Young Readers, an imprint of Penguin Putnam Books for Young Readers, a division of Penguin Putnam Inc. All rights reserved.

Front cover and interior design by Kathy Massaro
Interior illustrations by Maxie Chambliss

ISBN: 0-439-44992-8
Copyright © 2003 by Immacula A. Rhodes.
Published by Scholastic Inc.
All rights reserved.
Printed in the U.S.A.

3  4  5  6  7  8  9  10    40    09  08  07

# Contents

# About This Book

*W*inter is a season for celebrations! Every year, winter's cold, short days are brightened with the warmth and excitement of special religious and cultural holidays. Decorations color homes and communities, lights sparkle from windows and rooftops, music fills the air, and families gather to feast and exchange gifts. *Teaching About Winter Holidays With Favorite Picture Books* offers an array of activities created to help you and your students explore these celebrations—from Hanukkah, Las Posadas, and Christmas to Kwanzaa and Chinese New Year. Fresh, creative ideas related to fact-based, fictional, and humorous holiday books include activities that teach about, and extend beyond, the stories to incorporate interesting facts and the unique traditions and history of each holiday.

Each book unit includes a summary, story discussion idea, and a wide range of activities and projects designed to enrich students' learning across the curriculum. (Connections to the Language Arts and Social Studies standards are listed on page 6.) Sprinkled throughout the book, you'll find print and Internet resources for further reading, research, and holiday activities to supplement and extend learning.

As you and your students explore the books and suggested resources, you'll broaden your ideas and knowledge about a variety of winter holiday celebrations. Gather a stack of these holiday favorites, then join your students on an educational journey into the fascinating world of winter holidays.

## Getting Started

- Gather and read the books you plan to use for your holiday studies. Obtain multiple copies if possible.

- Prepare a winter-themed table display on which to feature your holiday books. Arrange other classroom areas to display book- and holiday-related projects.

- Use the resources listed on page 64 to become familiar with interesting facts and information about the winter holidays.

- Create a chart to show the different holidays, including when, where, why, and how they are celebrated. Also include symbols and words associated with each holiday. Use the chart to compare ways in which the different holidays are celebrated as well as how common elements—such as light, gifts, and feasts—are used in the celebrations.

- Arrange in advance to have guests visit the class to personally share the customs and traditions of different holiday celebrations. Some people you might invite include parents, family members, and school or community leaders.

◎ Preview the ideas in Creative Winter Holiday Crafts on page 60. Invite children to use any or all of these ideas to personalize their holiday celebrations.

◎ Set up an area for a Holiday Tapestry (see below). Encourage children to add to the display items that represent their personal holiday celebrations.

## Celebrating Diversity With a Holiday Tapestry

Most likely, your students observe a variety of winter holidays in ways that are unique and special to each individual and family. To highlight the diverse ways in which different holidays are observed, invite children to help weave this holiday tapestry by sharing their personal celebrations.

To prepare, cover a bulletin board with white paper. Then, as the class studies winter holidays, encourage students who observe each featured holiday to create or bring in items representing their personal and family celebrations. Invite children to share their items and holiday experiences with the class. Then have them display their items on the board. (If desired, you might invite all children to add to each holiday display.) The Tapestry Tips that accompany each book unit suggest items that students might share, such as photos, artwork, greeting cards, ornaments, and copies of songs. These tips are only guidelines—invite children to share their holiday celebrations in their own creative ways as well. At the end of your studies, the display will be a colorful tapestry of the diverse and unique ways students celebrate their holidays.

## Ways to Use the Holiday Tapestry

◎ As new items are added to your tapestry, ask children to compare them with items already on display. Have them discuss similarities and differences among common items as well as the variety of ways classmates celebrate the same holiday.

◎ Use the holiday tapestry to summarize the customs and traditions of each holiday and to compare all of the represented holidays.

◎ Generate writing prompts from items displayed on the tapestry. For example, you might have children write a description of an ornament or a comparison of two candleholders.

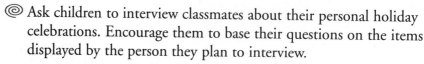

◎ Ask children to interview classmates about their personal holiday celebrations. Encourage them to base their questions on the items displayed by the person they plan to interview.

◎ Photograph the tapestry-in-progress and the completed tapestry. Add the pictures to your class album along with captions written by students.

◎ Invite children to create keepsake booklets that tell about ways class members celebrate the winter holidays. If desired, give them a photo of the completed tapestry to frame and attach to the cover of their booklets.

◎ Encourage children to use the holiday tapestry to explain holiday symbols and celebrations to class guests and visitors.

 Connections to the Language Arts and Social Studies Standards

The activities in this book are designed to support you in meeting the following standards outlined by the Mid-continent Research for Education and Learning (McREL), an organization that collects and synthesizes national and state K–12 curriculum standards.

## Language Arts

Uses the general skills and strategies of the reading process and reading skills and strategies to understand and interpret a variety of literary texts:

◆ Uses meaning clues to aid comprehension and make predictions about content

◆ Uses reading skills and strategies to understand a variety of familiar literary passages and texts, including fiction and nonfiction

◆ Knows main ideas or theme, setting, main characters, main events, sequence, and problems in stories

◆ Makes simple inferences regarding the order of events and possible outcomes

◆ Relates stories to personal experience

Source—(*Content Knowledge: A Compendium of Standards and Benchmarks for K–12 Education* (3rd ed.). (Mid-continent Research for Education and Learning, 2000)

Uses the general skills and strategies of the writing process:

◆ Uses writing and other methods to describe familiar persons, places, objects, or experiences

◆ Writes in a variety of forms or genres, including responses to literature

## Social Studies

Understands family life now and in the past, and family life in various places long ago:

◆ Understands personal family or cultural heritage through stories, songs, and celebrations

◆ Knows ways in which people share family beliefs and values (e.g., oral traditions, literature, songs, art, religions, community celebrations, mementos, food, language)

Understands selected attributes and historical developments in societies in Africa, the Americas, Asia, and Europe:

◆ Understands the main ideas found in folktales, stories of great heroism, fables, legends and myths from around the world that reflect the beliefs and ways of living of various cultures in times past

◆ Knows the holidays and ceremonies of different societies (e.g., Christmas celebrations, the Chinese New Year)

# On Hanukkah

BY CATHY GOLDBERG FISHMAN
(ATHENEUM BOOKS FOR YOUNG
READERS, 1998)

It's Hanukkah—a time for the family to share stories, eat potato latkes, play dreidel, and sing and dance. More important, it's a time to light the menorahs and remember the miracle of light from long ago. Told from a young girl's perspective, this Hanukkah story artfully weaves history and tradition together to describe a family's joyful celebration and the inspiration it receives from the menorah lights. Text and illustrations blend beautifully, creating a warm and gentle holiday tale.

Hanukkah is the Jewish holiday that commemorates the Jews' successful fight for religious freedom over 2,000 years ago. The holiday also commemorates a miracle that took place at that time: one day's supply of oil miraculously burned in the temple lamp for eight days. During the celebration of Hanukkah, families observe a number of traditions that represent their religious heritage—lighting the menorah, telling stories, preparing latkes, and playing dreidel. Use the book to review and discuss the origins and significance of these traditions. Then invite children to tell about some of their own family holiday traditions.

## Holiday Quick Fact

The word *Hanukkah* means "dedication." After fighting for their religious freedom, the Jews had to restore and rededicate their temple, which had been destroyed by enemies.

## Light With a Purpose (Social Studies and Language Arts)

In the story, on each night of Hanukkah, the child puts the menorah in the window as a light in the darkness, a light of hope, strength, faith, happiness, giving, knowledge, and freedom. Write each purpose for the light on chart paper. Then explain that, just as candles light up a room, children also light up their world in different ways—such as by helping, smiling, caring, and performing acts of kindness. Invite children to create personal menorahs to show how they shine light in the world.

**1** First, have them write "My light" and draw a self-portrait on a blank 3- by 5-inch notecard (placed vertically). This card will be used for the Shamash.

**2** On each of eight additional cards, students write and illustrate a way they shine their lights.

**3** Have them fold the nine cards in half lengthwise, decorate the front of each to represent a candle, and add a construction paper flame.

**4** Then ask children to draw a menorah on a 12- by 18-inch sheet of construction paper. Have them add their candles, gluing them to the page so they can be opened card-style. Invite children to share their menorahs with friends and family.

## How Many Candles? (Math)

During Hanukkah, candles are placed in a menorah from right to left and then lit from left to right. On the first night, one candle is put in the menorah. The Shamash is lit and then used to kindle, or light, the first candle. On the second night, a new candle is added. The Shamash is used to light the new candle and then the old one. In this manner, a new candle is added and burned for each night of Hanukkah until the entire menorah glows on the eighth night. Reinforce the menorah lighting procedure with this simple math activity. First, have small groups conduct imaginary candlelightings for each night of Hanukkah. Ask them to keep count of the lighted candles for each night, including the Shamash. Then have groups total their candle count and compare their final answers (the total is 44 candles).

### Holiday Quick Fact

A menorah is a candleholder for nine candles. The *Shamash*—a candle positioned higher in the center of the menorah—is used to light the other candles, which represent the eight days of Hanukkah.

## Class Menorah (Social Studies)

In the story, each person is described as a shining candle in the menorah of the family. Tell children that, similarly, they are all shining candles in the menorah of your class. Ask children to think about what makes them shine in class. Then have them cut out large paper flames to illustrate with self-portraits and label with the qualities they bring to the class. Create your own flame as well. Then have children pretend to be candles. Using an unlit tapered candle as the Shamash, pretend to light a child candle. When you do so, ask the child to stand, hold his or her flame overhead, and tell about how he or she lights up the class. When finished, have the child use the Shamash to light another child candle. Continue in this manner until every candle in the class has been lit. Later, top a construction paper candle with each flame to make a candle for each child. Then cluster the candles on a bulletin board to create a display for the menorah of your class.

## Hanukkah Quilt (Art and Social Studies)

The family in the story follows a tradition of decorating quilt squares during Hanukkah. In the same spirit, invite children to decorate squares to create a holiday quilt for your classroom. First, list on chart paper the Hanukkah symbols and their significance to the holiday. (These may come from the book or from students' personal experiences with the celebration.) Then provide various shapes and sizes of wrapping paper, including solid and patterned pieces. Ask each child to cut and glue the paper scraps to design one or more symbols on a 9-inch square of construction paper. Assemble the completed squares into a class quilt. Display the quilt and chart together in your classroom. Then invite children to point out and tell about their squares.

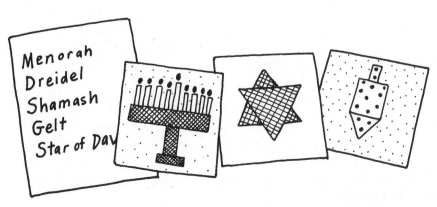

Menorah
Dreidel
Shamash
Gelt
Star of Dav

### Holiday Quick Fact

Often, Hanukkah gift wrap is blue and white and designed with the six-pointed Star of David (as well as other holiday symbols). These colors and the star are featured on the Israeli flag.

## Oil Paintings (Social Studies and Art)

In the Hanukkah miracle of light, one day's supply of oil burned in the temple for eight days! To commemorate this event, invite children to create these stained-glass oil paintings. To begin, ask them to sketch a Hanukkah-related drawing on a paper plate. Then have students paint their pictures with watercolors. After the paintings dry, have them use cotton balls to apply a light coat of vegetable oil over their pictures. Set aside the plates for a few days to allow the oil to soak in. Help children attach yarn hangers to their pictures and hang them in a classroom window.

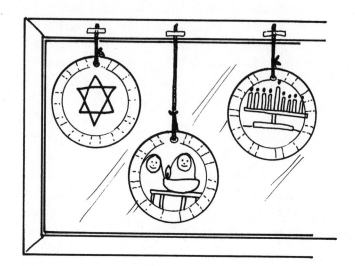

## Hanukkah Moon Observations (Science)

Unlike the western 365-day calendar, the Jewish calendar is based on the cycle of the moon, with each month beginning on a new moon. Hanukkah is observed near the end of the month of Kislev in the Jewish calendar. Ask children to predict the moon phase for this time of the month. Then ask them to observe and draw the moon on the first and last nights of Hanukkah. Have students compare the two drawings and describe the differences. What happens to the moon? Explain that during this time in Kislev—the month-end—the moon is in a crescent phase. Each night of Hanukkah, the moon gets smaller, until finally it disappears from view. The moon soon reappears as a crescent to begin the next month in the calendar.

## Acts of Giving (Social Studies)

On each day of Hanukkah, many families exchange gifts. Another holiday tradition, called *tzedaka*, is that of helping people in need, either by giving time, effort, or money. Designate one day during Hanukkah as a special Giving Day in your class. Invite children to prepare simple gifts for classmates (cards, certificates, drawings, poems, or crafts). Also, make a class decision about a project to help the needy in your community. This project might involve collecting food or money to donate to a charitable organization. Prepare and send home notes to parents to tell about your Giving Day. Then, on the appointed day, have children bring in and distribute their gifts and donations. If your class took a collection for a charity, you might also plan a field trip to deliver the donations to the designated organization.

## Related Reading

◆ **Grandma's Latkes** by Malka Drucker (Harcourt Brace Jovanovich, 1992). Grandma explains the history and traditions of Hanukkah as she and Molly prepare latkes for their family celebration.

◆ **A Great Miracle Happened There: A Chanukah Story** by Karla Kuskin (Willa Perlman Books, 1993). When Henry spends the first night of Chanukah with his friend, he participates in the lighting of the menorah and learns about the Jews' fight for religious freedom and the miracle of the oil that lasted eight days.

◆ **One Candle** by Eve Bunting (Joanna Cotler Books, 2002). Every Hanukkah, Grandma reminisces about the courage, strength, and determination of a group of girls to honor Hanukkah while imprisoned in a concentration camp. Then, just as she did so long ago, Grandma lights a potato candle to represent the light of hope.

◆ **Our Eight Nights of Hanukkah** by Michael J. Rosen (Holiday House, 2000). A Jewish family enjoys its Hanukkah customs of singing songs, telling the story of Judah Maccabee, making latkes, giving to the needy, going to the synagogue, exchanging gifts, and spending time together.

◆ **Pearl's Eight Days of Chanukah** by Jane Breskin Zalben (Simon & Schuster, 1998). Pearl fears the worst when she learns that her cousins will be spending all eight nights of Chanukah with her family. But participating in holiday activities together makes Pearl realize that she truly enjoys their company. Includes crafts, recipes, and songs.

Tapestry Tips

To help weave the class holiday tapestry, you might have children add:

● a photo or drawing of a menorah used in their personal Hanukkah celebrations.

● a memento representing a special holiday tradition, such as a photo of a family quilt, a piece of gelt, or a sample of holiday gift wrap.

● a photo of their family celebrating Hanukkah.

● an illustrated poem or story about how they use the history of the holiday in their family celebration.

# Hooray for Hanukkah!

BY FRAN MANUSHKIN
(RANDOM HOUSE, 2001)

**F**rom the first night of Hanukkah to the last, a menorah describes the joyful activities surrounding a family's eight-night celebration. Cheerfully expressing its will to be brighter after each candlelighting, the menorah finally reaches the highlight of the holiday. With its eighth and final candle lit and the lights turned off, the menorah glows its brightest as the family soaks in memories to last the year. Hooray for Hanukkah!

Throughout the story, the menorah tells about activities that surround it during the family's Hanukkah celebration. Review the story with students to find ways in which the menorah describes (or implies) its own participation and enjoyment in the festivities. For instance, it attracts visitors, it glows, it lights up eyes and faces, its flames dance, and it pushes the darkness away. Write these on chart paper. Then invite children to add other ways in which the menorah might participate and express its pleasure in the celebration. Afterward, ask children to imagine they are the menorah. Which activity would they enjoy most? How would they participate in the activity?

## Personal Perspectives (Language Arts)

This Hanukkah story is told from a menorah's perspective. Explain that to tell the story, the author imagined the menorah could think and feel as a person. On chart paper, write "menorah," as well as other symbols of Hanukkah, such as the Shamash, a dreidel, gelt, and latkes. Ask students to select a symbol from the list. Then have them write and illustrate a holiday story from that object's perspective. Ask them to title their stories, create covers, and bind the pages into a book. Then invite children to share their stories with each other. Alternatively, children might retell the story from one family member's perspective—or even from the cat's point of view!

## Folding Menorah (Language Arts and Social Studies)

Invite children to make this special menorah to use in retelling the story to family and friends.

**1** To begin, students fold two sheets of 8 1/2- by 11-inch white copy paper accordion-style, as shown.

**2** Then they cut out the candle pattern on page 15, trace it onto each of the folded papers, cut out the shapes through all thicknesses, and unfold the resulting candle chain. (Make sure children do not cut through the folds at the candle bases.)

**3** Next, students cut out the Shamash pattern. They glue each candle chain to an end of the Shamash to create a menorah.

**4** Children then color the Shamash and write the book title on its flame.

**5** Starting from left to right, they label the other candles with "first night, second night," and so on. Then students write an event from the story on each corresponding candle. When finished, they accordion-fold their menorahs with the first candle on top.

To use, children retell the story, unfolding their menorahs and showing each candle as the events of the story unfold.

*Related Reading*

◆ **Eight Days of Hanukkah** by Harriet Ziefert (Viking, 1997). Each turn of the page shows an additional candle in the menorah and introduces a different Hanukkah ritual, such as lighting candles, telling stories, and cooking latkes. Colorful collage illustrations complement the lively text.

◆ **Hanukkah: A Counting Book in English, Hebrew, and Yiddish** by Emily Sper (Scholastic, 2001). Bold illustrations and die-cut pages feature color-coded English, Hebrew, and Yiddish spellings and pronunciations for the numbers one through eight. Each spread also shows different Hanukkah symbols and the corresponding number of candles for the menorah.

◆ **Hanukkah Lights, Hanukkah Nights** by Leslie Kimmelman (HarperCollins, 1992). Lighting the menorah, playing dreidel, and enjoying family togetherness are a few of the Hanukkah traditions highlighted in this beautifully illustrated introduction to the Jewish holiday.

## Holiday Quick Fact

Latkes and jelly doughnuts, called *sufganiyot*, are favorite Hanukkah foods. Both are fried in oil to symbolize the oil that burned for eight days and nights during the first Hanukkah.

## Tapestry Tips

To help weave the class holiday tapestry, you might have children add:

- an illustrated story about their personal experiences celebrating Hanukkah.

- a candle from the menorah along with an account of its role in the holiday celebration.

- a recipe for latkes or other favorite holiday food.

- a photo or drawing of their favorite Hanukkah activity.

## Cooperative Class Latkes (Cooking and Social Skills)

In the story, the family worked together to make potato latkes. In the same spirit of cooperation, invite children to distribute the responsibilities listed below and work together to mix up a batch of this simplified recipe for latkes. (You might copy the steps below onto chart paper or sentence strips and place in a pocket chart.) Afterward, you or another adult heat oil in a frying pan and drop the mixture by the spoonful into the oil. When brown on one side, flip the latkes and brown them on the other side. Drain the latkes on paper towels, then serve them to your class with sour cream or applesauce. (Check for food allergies before serving to children.)

### Potato Latkes

(makes 24 mini-latkes)

1. Wash 6 large potatoes.
2. Peel the potatoes.
3. Grate the potatoes into a bowl.
4. Drain the excess liquid from the potatoes.
5. In another bowl, beat two eggs.
6. Add the grated potatoes to the eggs. Mix them together.
7. Stir in two tablespoons of flour.
8. Stir in one teaspoon of salt.

## Even Brighter (Science)

Ask children to explain the menorah's repeated lines, "I am bright, but I *could* be brighter." To help them understand the menorah's meaning, turn off the lights. Then light a candle (or use an electric or battery-operated candle). How bright is the candlelight? Ask children to predict what will happen when a second candle is lit. After lighting another candle, have children share their observations. Continue lighting candles, one at a time, until nine are burning at the same time. What happens to the brightness of the light as each candle is lit?

# Folding
# Menorah

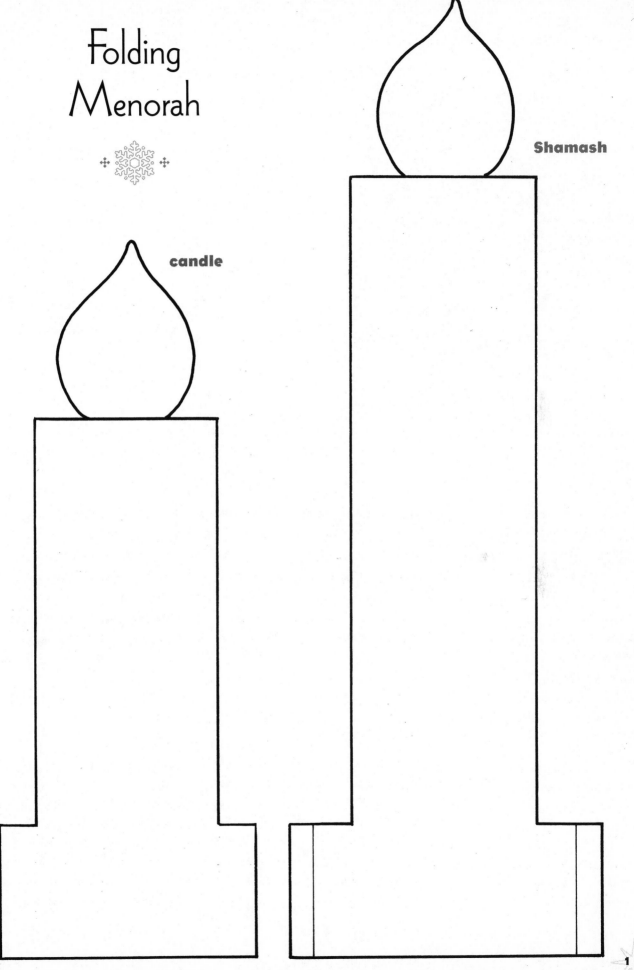

**Shamash**

**candle**

# Runaway Dreidel!

BY LESLÉA NEWMAN
(HENRY HOLT AND COMPANY, 2002)

While his family prepares for Hanukkah, a boy's shiny new dreidel begins to spin out of control. Spinning down the stairs, onto the streets, and out of the city, the dreidel leads the boy and his family on a cross-country chase. But when it reaches the sea's edge, the boy is sure that he'll soon have his toy back in his hand. Much to everyone's surprise, though, the dreidel has one more leg of its journey to complete before it stops. Boldly colored illustrations playfully accent this humorous holiday tale.

Use this tale to get students' creative storytelling juices flowing. After discussing the dreidel's adventures and how they distracted from and added to the family's Hanukkah celebration, ask children to think of their own imaginary holiday-related adventures. Invite them to briefly share their ideas with the class. Then send students to the writing center to develop, write, and illustrate their stories.

## Dreidel Game (Social Studies)

Many traditional Jewish items, foods, and customs are woven into the telling of *Runaway Dreidel!* Invite children to refer to the book to learn Hanukkah-related facts while playing this modified dreidel game. Follow these directions for each playing group.

**1** To prepare, cut out the fact cards and spinner on page 19. Fold the fact cards in half and place them in a small bag. Glue the spinner onto a piece of tagboard. Laminate, if desired.

**2** Use a paper fastener to loosely attach a small paper-clip spinner to the dreidel spinner.

**3** Place the bag of fact cards on a table along with a bowl (or paper cup.)

**4** Before play starts, review the Hebrew letters and their meanings on the dreidel spinner (see right).

◎ To play, a caller distributes five dried beans to each of three or four players.

◎ Each player puts one bean in the bowl.

◎ The caller picks a fact card and reads it to the first player. The player must decide whether the statement is true or false. If he or she answers correctly, the player spins the dreidel and follows the direction that lands faceup. If his or her answer is incorrect, the fact card goes back into the bag, and the next player takes a turn.

◎ Players take turns in this manner until one player wins all the beans in the bowl. (When a player is out of counters, he or she is out of the game.) Or play can continue for a given amount of time, after which the player with the most beans wins. After the game, give each player a piece of gelt (chocolates wrapped to look like money) to enjoy.

*Nun* means "take none." The player does nothing and the next player takes a turn.

*Gimel* means "take all." Any time a player spins *Gimel*, the player takes all of the counters. All players must put one into the pot before the game can continue.

*Heh* (hay) means "take half." If a player rolls *Heh*, the player takes half of the counters from the pot. (If there's an odd number of counters in the pot, the player takes one extra.)

*Shin* means "put one in." The player puts one counter into the pot.

## Spinning a Tale (Social Studies and Language Arts)

The runaway dreidel led the boy and his family on a cross-country adventure. Have children use information from the story to map the dreidel's path on large construction paper, sequencing its locations by number. Then invite students to use their maps to spin off their own versions of the tale.

## Scientific Spins (Science)

The boy's dreidel spun across floors, streets, grass, and a variety of other terrain before spinning off into the sky. Ask children if a dreidel can *really* spin that easily on any surface. To test their responses, equip small groups with paper, pencil, a stopwatch, and a dreidel (or top). Have the groups list surfaces around the school on which to test-spin their dreidels (a tile floor, carpet, sidewalk, grass, sand, and so on). Then ask them to write their predictions about whether or not the dreidel will spin on each surface, and how long it will spin. Finally, have students spin the dreidel three times on each surface, recording its spinning time for each trial and observations about how it spins. After children have conducted their experiments, invite groups to share and compare their results.

**Tapestry Tips**

To help weave the class holiday tapestry, you might have children add:

- a photo or drawing of their favorite dreidel, or a real handmade dreidel.

- rules for playing dreidel.

- the symbols on a dreidel and an explanation of their meanings.

- the words to a favorite dreidel song or a copy of their favorite holiday song.

- an item or drawing, such as a holiday card or gift wrapping, showing the Star of David.

## Related Reading

For more Hanukkah adventures, share these magical tales:

◆ *Latkes, Latkes, Good to Eat: A Chanukah Story* by Naomi Howland (Clarion Books, 1999). On the first night of Chanukah, poor, hungry Sadie gives an old woman her firewood and is rewarded with a magic latke-making pan. The pan always works for Sadie, but when her curious brothers try to use it, latke-laced chaos erupts in the village.

◆ *The Magic Dreidels* by Eric A. Kimmel (Holiday House, 1996). When Jacob shows Fruma Sarah his magic dreidels, the greedy woman tricks the boy and keeps them for herself. That is, until one dreidel spins out a surprise that makes Fruma Sarah itch to return the dreidels to their rightful owner.

◆ *The Magic Menorah: A Modern Chanukah Tale* by Jane Breskin Zalben (Simon & Schuster, 2001). When Stanley cleans an old menorah, a genie appears and grants him three wishes. Desiring fame, fortune, and happiness, the boy discovers that wishes can be answered in surprising and unanticipated ways. Hebrew and Yiddish words are sprinkled throughout this chapter-book story.

◆ *Moishe's Miracle: A Hanukkah Story* by Laura Krauss Melmed (HarperCollins, 2000). While sleeping in the cowshed to escape his wife's scolding, the generous Moishe receives a special gift—a magic pan that makes latkes. As he does with all things, the kind man shares his good fortune with his neighbors, but his greedy wife has other ideas for the pan.

◆ *The Runaway Latkes* by Leslie Kimmelman (Albert Whitman & Company, 2000). In this cumulative Hanukkah tale based on "The Gingerbread Man," one character after another joins the chase as Rebecca tries to catch her runaway latkes.

# Dreidel Game

A menorah holds nine candles. (True)

Family members exchange gifts during Hanukkah. (True)

Challah is bread that can be bought at a bakery. (True)

Chocolates wrapped to look like money are called gelt. (True)

All family members can participate in a Hanukkah celebration. (True)

A six-pointed star is a symbol of Hanukkah. (True)

**Spinner**

Nun — Take none.

Gimel — Take all.

Shin — Put one in.

Heh (hay) — Take half.

**Hanukkah Fact Cards**

A recipe for latkes includes eggs. (True)

All the candles in a menorah are lit on the first day of Hanukkah. (False)

A dreidel is a four-sided toy. (True)

The hora is a special Hanukkah game. (False)

Families gather for feasts and fun on Hanukkah. (True)

A dreidel can spin nonstop for hours. (False)

A dreidel has Hebrew letters on it. (True)

Hanukkah is celebrated only in Jewish temples. (False)

The Shamash is the last candle on the menorah to be lit. (False)

Music cannot be played during Hanukkah. (False)

Babka is the name of a dreidel game. (False)

A dreidel is a six-pointed spinning star. (False)

Latkes are made from grated apples. (False)

Only one candle burns during the Hanukkah holiday. (False)

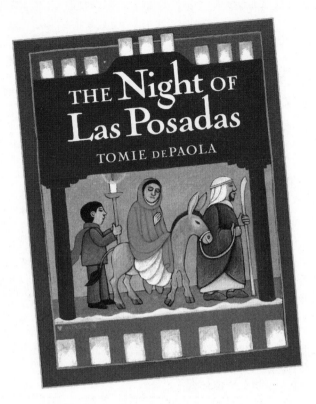

# The Night of Las Posadas

BY TOMIE dePAOLA
(PENGUIN PUTMAN BOOKS
FOR YOUNG READERS, 1999)

It's time for Las Posadas, and Lupe and Roberto have been chosen to play the parts of Mary and Joseph in search of shelter on the night of Jesus' birth. On their way to the celebration, the couple makes a quick visit to see Sister Angie, the longtime organizer of the celebration, who is too sick to attend the festivities this year. But as they head towards town, now aglow with festive faces and *farolitos*, their truck gets stuck in a snowstorm. With Sister Angie absent, and Mary and Joseph stranded, will Las Posadas go on? The author-illustrator's distinctive art and storytelling style create a magical blend in this tale of a Las Posadas miracle.

Explain that Las Posadas is a nine-day celebration, lasting from December 16 to 24, that focuses on the biblical story of Mary and Joseph's visit to Bethlehem at the time of Jesus' birth. Las Posadas is celebrated in Mexico, Spain, and several southwestern states in the United States, including New Mexico, Texas, Arizona, and California. Locate these countries and states on a map. Afterward, ask children to think about how the story might be told from one of the characters' perspectives. Have them imagine they are Sister Angie, Lupe, Roberto, Mary, Joseph, or even the donkey. Invite children to share their versions of the story with the class. Later, children might put on costumes and act out the actual story as well as their character-perspective versions.

## Las Posadas Pilgrimage (Social Studies)

In the reenactment at the Plaza, Mary and Joseph are four times denied entrance to an inn. Finally, the door opens and the *peregrinos* (pilgrims) enter to commemorate the birth of Jesus. Children can experience their own Las Posadas adventures with this game. First, color, cut out, and laminate the cards (below) and the game board (page 23). Place the cards facedown on the game board. For game markers, draw a face on several lima beans with a permanent marker. Then divide the class into groups of two to three children and have them follow these steps to play the game:

◎ Each player places a pilgrim game marker on a blank space. In turn, players toss a penny and move according to how it lands: Heads moves two spaces and tails moves one. Players can move in any direction along the path. Players follow the directions on any corresponding space.

◎ When they land on a house, players ask, "May we come in?" and then pick a card. If the card says "No!," the player places the card on the house and moves to a space on either side of the house. When reaching a house with a "No!" card, players jump over the house to the next space. When the "Yes!" card is drawn, that player ends the game with a win.

◎ At the end of each game, invite players to enjoy a favorite Las Posadas treat—*bischochitos* (sugar cookies)!

Holiday Quick Fact

The end of a Las Posadas celebration is a festive occasion. Often, children take turns swinging a stick at a suspended *piñata*—a papier-maché container filled with candy, fruit, and gifts. When the piñata breaks, the goodies spill out and children scramble to collect their favorites.

| Yes! | No! | No! |
| --- | --- | --- |
| No! | No! | No! |
| No! | No! | No! |

**cards**

To help weave the class holiday tapestry, you might have children add:

- a photo of their personal participation in a Las Posadas celebration.

- an illustrated, personal account of their Las Posadas experiences.

- a recipe for tamales, bischochitos, or other favorite holiday food.

- a photo, drawing, or miniature model of a piñata along with a description of how it is used in a holiday celebration.

- a paper bag farolito.

## Fancy Farolitos (Language Arts and Social Studies)

In a Las Posadas procession, Mary and Joseph, along with other caroling peregrinos, may visit homes to seek shelter for up to nine nights. The homes represent *posadas*, or inns, and are often lit up with *luminarias*—or bonfires—and *farolitos*, small bags with candles. Light up students' writing skills with these fancy farolitos. First, write Spanish and English words related to Las Posadas on a chart. Then have students copy and illustrate the words on white paper bags, adding a festive touch by gluing on scraps of colorful gift wrap. Then ask children to create their own Las Posadas stories, lacing Spanish words into their tales as much as possible. To share, have them put a lit flashlight, standing on end, inside their farolitos. Then have them read their stories. Encourage children to also share the stories with their families by the light of their fancy farolitos.

## Related Reading

- ◆ *Carlos, Light the Farolito* by Jean Ciavonne (Clarion Books, 1995). With his grandfather and parents not yet home, the shy and frightened Carlos must play the role of the mean innkeeper when the Las Posadas procession comes to his house.

- ◆ *The Farolitos of Christmas* by Rudolfo Anaya (Hyperion Books for Children, 1995). Luz worries that her ill grandfather will be unable to light the Christmas luminarias for the holiday celebration. Determined to help her grandfather keep his promise to the community, Luz makes little lanterns, or farolitos, to light the path for the pilgrims.

- ◆ *Nine Days to Christmas* by Marie Hall Ets and Aurora Lambastida (Viking, 1987). Five-year-old Ceci gets caught up in the excitement and anticipation of picking out a piñata and participating in her first posadas.

- ◆ *Pancho's Piñata* by Stefan Czernecki (Hyperion Books for Children, 1992). After freeing a star from a cactus on Christmas Eve, young Pancho receives the gift of happiness. Years later, Pancho creates a star-shaped piñata and fills it with goodies so that he can share his happiness with the children of his town.

- ◆ *Too Many Tamales* by Gary Soto (G. P. Putnam's Sons, 1993). Maria secretly tries on Mom's diamond ring while helping to make the Christmas tortillas. Later, suspecting that the ring slipped off her finger and into a tamale, she solicits her cousins' help to find it before Mom discovers that the ring is missing.

# Las Posadas Pilgrimage

## game board

Shortcut. Take another turn.

Place cards here.

Dark path. Lose turn.

Sing carols. Move ahead 1.

Burro trots. Move ahead 1.

Snowdrift. Lose turn.

Bright farolitos. Move ahead 1.

*Teaching About Winter Holidays With Favorite Picture Books*
Scholastic Teaching Resources

# The Last Straw

BY FREDRICK H. THURY
(CHARLESBRIDGE, 1998)

In spite of his aching joints and other pains, the proud Hoshmakaka accepts the task of carrying the wise men's gifts to the new baby king in Bethlehem. With three younger camels at his side, each in awe of the old camel's boast of extraordinary strength, Hoshmakaka foolishly agrees to carry one gift after another from well-wishers along the way. When he most fears that his strength will fail him, the camel sights Bethlehem beneath the shining star—and he knows he can make it if he can just keep moving! Suddenly, a small child appears to make one final request of the overburdened camel. With this last gift onboard, Hoshmakaka reaches his limit, sinking humbly to his knees beside the baby—where he miraculously discovers the true purpose of his journey.

Discuss the meaning of the phrases *This is the last straw* and *the straw that broke the camel's back.* How do these relate to the story? To help children understand how Hoshmakaka got into his predicament, have them list the camel's character traits on chart paper. Ask them to check the traits that helped create his problem (boastful, proud, determined, foolish). Then have students underline the traits that motivated him to complete his task (determined, proud, patient, caring, obedient). Can they describe how some of the same traits played a part in both creating and resolving Hoshmakaka's problems? Invite students to tell about times in which they experienced problems as a result of boasting. What character traits did they apply to resolve the problems?

## Gift-Bearing Camel Puppet (Language Arts and Art)

Christians believe that Jesus, born in Bethlehem over 2,000 years ago, is the son of God. At the time of his birth, a group of wise men traveled many miles to worship the baby king and to give him gifts. Invite students to make this camel puppet to use in retelling the story of Hoshmakaka's journey with the wise men. First, children color and cut out the camel and gift patterns (page 28). Then they cut out one more camel pattern. To make the puppet, students glue the two camels together, leaving an opening at the hump to serve as a pocket. While the glue is still wet, they trap a yarn tail and four craft stick legs between the camel patterns, as shown. Then they glue a 1/2- by 3-inch strip of tagboard to each gift. To use, children retell the story, inserting one gift after another into the camel's hump as the story progresses. If desired, children can make additional props to expand the story or create their own version.

## Bright Star of Bethlehem (Social Studies and Art)

Hoshmakaka and the wise men followed a special star into Bethlehem to find the baby Jesus. Invite children to create a star candle to commemorate this event. To begin, students color and cut out the candle and flame patterns (right). Then they glue the star pattern (page 28) to tagboard and cut it out. Next, they label the points of the star with words related to the Christmas story (*gifts, star, stable, wise men, baby, shepherds, angels,* and so on). To make a stand-up candle, children fold the candle pattern where indicated and glue the ends together, trapping the flame between them. To complete their star candles, students glue the candles onto their stars. Ask students to use their star candles to tell about the Christmas story. They can also take them home to use as holiday table centerpieces. They can display their stars flat on the table or bend back each point to create a raised stand for the candle.

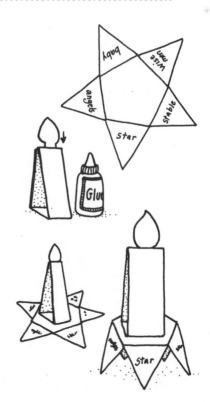

**flame pattern**

Glue here.

Fold up here.

Fold up here.

**candle pattern**

**25**

## Where Is Bethlehem? (Social Studies)

Many traveled far to see the newborn king in Bethlehem, a small town located five miles south of Israel's capital, Jerusalem. Ask children to find Jerusalem on a large world map and mark it with a star sticker. What landforms are found in this area of the world? Would students like to visit Jerusalem (or Bethlehem)? Why or why not? How far would they have to travel? To find out, have children use yarn, a ruler, and the map scale to determine the distance.

## Camel Caravan (Science)

Camels were used as work animals by people of biblical times, and still are today. To learn more about *dromedaries* (camels), ask children to research camel facts in books, encyclopedias, and on the Internet. (Informational Web sites include **www.arab.net/camels**; **http://vanishingspecies.net/animals/camel/index.htm**; and **www.livingdesert.org/sgcamel.html**.) Then have students color and cut out enlarged copies of the camel pattern (page 28), adding a tail and legs to complete their camels. Ask them to write a few camel facts on their animals. Finally, display the camels in a line to create a caravan of facts.

## Gifts Fit for a King (Social Studies and Art)

The wise men traveled far to offer the baby Jesus gifts fit for a king—gold, frankincense, and myrrh. In the story, others also brought gifts, from practical (milk) to personal (jewels) to proper for royalty (silks). Have children imagine what kind of gifts they would offer a king. Then have them create these unique gift packages filled with their imaginary offerings.

**1** To begin, ask children to glue two 5- by 14 1/2-inch tagboard strips together to make one long strip.

**2** Have them accordion-fold the strip into six equal sections, stretch it open, draw a gift on each panel, and then refold the strips.

**3** Instruct students to glue two 24-inch lengths of ribbon on the back panel, crossing the ribbons at the center, as shown.

**4** After the glue has dried, help students tie the ribbons in a bow across the front of their gift packages.

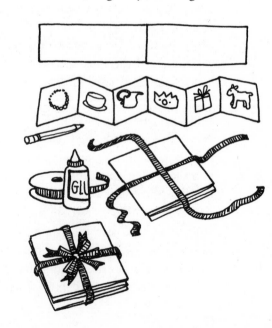

## A Heavy Burden (Science and Math)

Hoshmakaka carried many heavy gifts to Bethlehem—a chest of gold, pillars of oak, bags of grain, and gallons of wine, to name a few. To sample the weight of the load carried by the camel, have children weigh a gallon jug of water (to represent a gallon of wine). Next, have them remove the jug and stack books onto a scale until it reaches the weight of the jug. Instruct them to place the books in a sturdy box or large plastic storage container, weigh another stack of books, and add them to the box until it holds 20 stacks. Tell students that the box now holds the same weight as the wine carried by Hoshmakaka. Challenge them to move the box. How easy or hard is the task? To find the weight of the books in the box, help children multiply the weight of one jug of water by 20. Next, have students weigh other objects representing gifts from the story, such as a shoe box filled with rolled coins (gold), bundled stacks of long wood blocks (oak pillars), and a few bags of flour (ground corn). Each time, ask students to place the objects in the box, add the weight to that of the other items in the box, and then try to move the box.

Related Reading

◆ **B Is for Bethlehem: A Christmas Alphabet** by Isabel Wilner (Dutton Children's Books, 1990). In simple rhyming text, Christmas words are presented in alphabetical order to tell the nativity story.

◆ **The Christmas Star** by Marcus Pfister (North-South Books, 1993). Shepherds, wise men, and others follow a sparkling star until it comes to rest over the stable housing the holy child.

◆ **The Little Boy's Christmas Gift** by John Speirs (Harry N. Abrams, 2001). Told that he's too young to give a gift fit for a king, a boy secretly follows the wise men's caravan to the stable where the baby king rests. After all the gifts have been presented, the boy steps forward to offer a special gift—a beautifully decorated tree representing the many who journeyed to honor the new king.

◆ **The Stable Where Jesus Was Born** by Rhonda Gowler Greene (Atheneum Books for Young Readers, 1999). The excitement and anticipation of the birth of Jesus is captured in cumulative, rhyming text that describes the stable where he was born, his parents, the shepherds' visit, and the angels' appearance.

◆ **The Story of the Three Wise Kings** by Tomie dePaola (G. P. Putnam's Sons, 1983). Believing that the appearance of a new star symbolized the birth of a great king, three wise kings follow the brilliant light to Bethlehem, where they present gifts to the baby king.

◆ **This Is the Star** by Joyce Dunbar (Harcourt Brace & Company, 1996). A star in the night leads shepherds and wise men to the Christ child born to be king. Cumulative text coupled with extraordinary illustrations tells the nativity story in a rhythmic, reverent tone.

Tapestry Tips

To help weave the class holiday tapestry, you might have children add:

● a photo, drawing, miniature model, or holiday card featuring a nativity scene.

● the words to their favorite song about the birth of Jesus.

● an ornament related to the Christmas story, such as an angel, star, or nativity figure.

● a photo of their personal participation in a reenactment of the Christmas story.

● an illustrated poem or story about how they use the Christmas story in their family celebration.

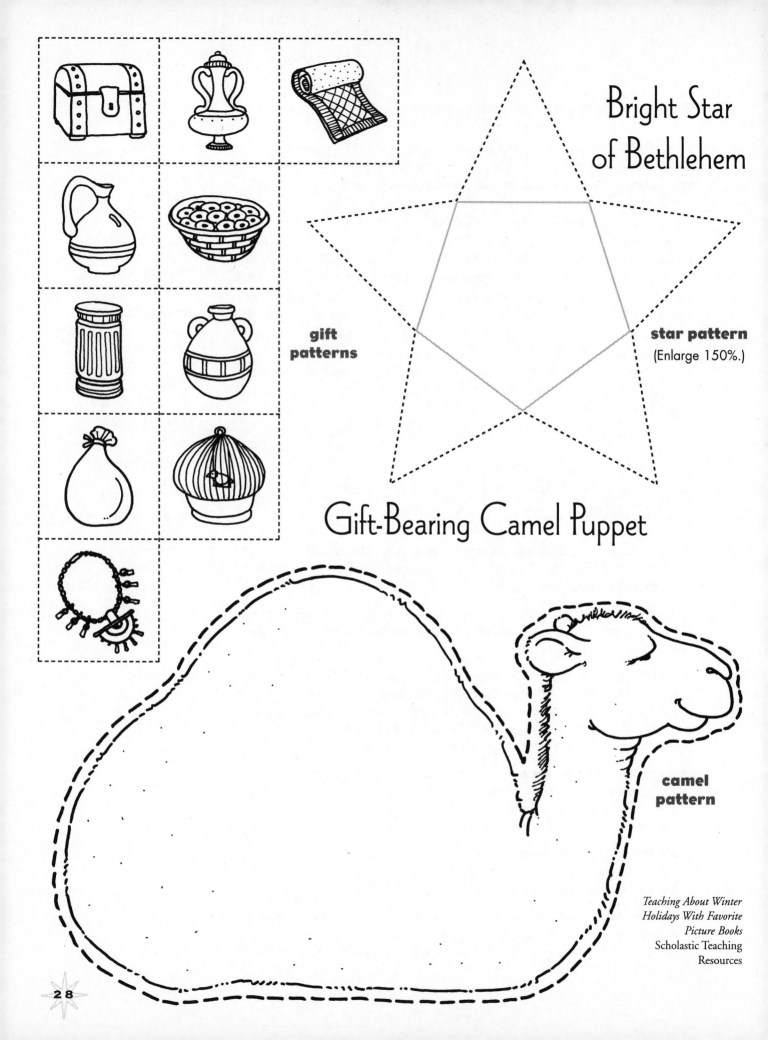

**gift patterns**

# Bright Star of Bethlehem

**star pattern**
(Enlarge 150%.)

# Gift-Bearing Camel Puppet

**camel pattern**

*Teaching About Winter Holidays With Favorite Picture Books*
Scholastic Teaching Resources

# Santa Who?

BY GAIL GIBBONS
(MORROW JUNIOR BOOKS, 1999)

How did Santa Claus become the well-loved, jolly gift-giver that we know today? The legend of this famous Christmas symbol began hundreds of years ago. Early Santa figures were called by different names in different cultures, with each sporting a distinctive look and carrying out different gift-giving rituals. From the first Saint Nicholas to the Dutch Sinter Cleas to the media-inspired American Santa Claus, this book explores the faces, facts, and folklore that have influenced the image of the beloved modern-day Santa Claus.

After reading the story, list the countries mentioned in the book. Then write the gift-giver's name for each listed country on a separate sticky note. Invite volunteers to find the countries on a large world map or globe and then attach the corresponding sticky notes to each one. Explain that today's Santa Claus has been shaped by many different cultures over the years. Have children discuss some ways in which figures and customs of the past have influenced the current image of Santa Claus.

## Gift-Giver Comparison Chart (Social Studies)

| | Saint Nicholas | Father Christmas | Befana | Santa Claus | Elf | Christkindl |
|---|---|---|---|---|---|---|
| **Country** | Turkey | England | Italy | United States | Sweden, Denmark, Norway | Germany, Spain, France, Italy |
| **Customs** | Left secret gifts for children. Rode white horse. Wore bishop's robe. | | Got lost bringing gifts to Christ. Still looking for him, she leaves gifts for children. | | Left gifts for children. | Brought Christ bundles (gifts). |
| **Other** | | | | Children left out rice pudding. | | Also called Nino Jesus, Petit Noel, Gesu Bambino |

Create this chart with students to compare the names, appearances, rituals, and other interesting facts about different gift-givers throughout history. To begin, divide a chart into six columns. Enlarge, color, and cut out the patterns (page 33), then attach one to the top of each column. If desired, include additional columns on the chart and add sketches of other gift-givers (such as Sinter Cleas and Babushka). Label the left side of the chart as shown. Then have small groups use the book and other resources to research and fill in the chart with information about their selected gift-givers. Afterward, have students use the chart to discuss and compare characteristics of the different gift-givers.

## Mystery Bags (Social Studies and Language Arts)

Challenge students' Santa savvy with clues from these mystery bags. To prepare, glue each gift-giver pattern (page 33) to a notecard. Write the gift-giver's name on each card, then write the name again on a separate card. Tape each picture card to the bottom of a holiday-decorated paper bag. Then label strips of paper with clues about each gift-giver, and drop these into the corresponding bags. To use, student partners take turns removing and reading clues from the bags. Together, they decide which gift-giver is described by each bag's clues and then place the corresponding name card with the bag. To check their work, children compare the name cards to the picture cards on the bottom of the bags.

## Gift-Giver Gazette (Language Arts and Social Studies)

Hear ye! Hear ye! Children can learn all the news about gift-givers in this special edition newspaper. To make the special edition, create a newspaper banner labeled "Gift-Giver Gazette" and glue it over the banner of a local newspaper. Then invite children to select a gift-giver from the book (or draw a name from a basket). Ask them to research, write, and illustrate articles about their gift-givers. If desired, they can also use the corresponding gift-giver patterns (page 33) with their work. When completed, glue students' articles and pictures onto the pages of the newspaper. Have children share their articles, then add the newspaper to your reading center for them to enjoy during independent reading times.

## It's Great to Give! Games (Language Arts and Social Skills)

In the spirit of giving, invite children to play these games using the gift-giver patterns on page 33:

◎ **Scavenger Gift Hunt** Wrap a gift for the class—perhaps a book for the reading center or new markers for the art center. Hide the gift somewhere in your school, such as the principal's office or library. Then enlarge, color, and cut out the patterns. On the backs, write clues that lead to other clues, and finally to the hidden gift. Hide each clue in a strategic location around the school. Give children the first clue and challenge them to find the gift.

◎ **Gift-Giver Match-Up** Separately wrap a small shoe box and its lid. Cut out four sets of patterns, glue each one to a notecard, then shuffle the cards. To use, a small group places the cards facedown. The first player picks two cards. If the cards match, the player keeps the pair and takes another turn. If the cards don't match, the player returns one card to the table, puts the other in the wrapped box, and passes the box to the next player. This player "unwraps" the card in the box (i.e., takes it out of the box), and then tries to find its match by picking a card from the table. If a match is not found, the player returns the cards to their places and passes the box to the next player. The game continues, with the "wrapped" card remaining in play until a player finds its match. At this time, the player repeats the procedure for the first play of the game. The game ends when all the matches have been made.

In addition to leaving gifts in stockings, Santa also leaves them under the Christmas tree. The tree-decorating tradition celebrated today in the United States originated in 16th-century Germany and spread to this country in the 1820s. Martin Luther, the Protestant reformer, was the first to light candles on an indoor Christmas tree, attempting to duplicate the beauty of starlight through the branches of outdoor trees.

**Tapestry Tips**

To help weave the class holiday tapestry, you might have children add:

- personal letters to or from Santa.
- the words to their favorite song about Santa Claus.
- a picture of a personal visit with Santa Claus.
- a summary of their favorite book about Santa (or the actual book).

## Stuffed Stockings (Math)

The Dutch-inspired tradition of filling stockings with goodies is now a common Christmas practice in America. Place several different-size stockings and a supply of stocking stuffers (such as small toys, nuts, or miniature candy bars) in your math center. Then have children visit the center to practice making estimations. To begin, they pick a stocking, estimate the number of stocking stuffers that will fit in it, and write their estimate on a sticky note. Then they stuff the stocking, empty it, and count the stocking stuffers. Was their estimate too high, too low, or just right?

Related Reading

- *Baboushka: A Christmas Folktale From Russia* by Arthur Scholey (Candlewick Press, 2001). Too busy to join the three kings on their journey to find the newborn king, Baboushka travels alone to Bethlehem only to find that the baby is gone.

- *How Santa Got His Job* by Stephen Krensky (Aladdin, 2002). Trying his hand at a variety of jobs, including sweeping chimneys, delivering packages, caring for zoo animals, and working at a circus, Santa Claus discovers his dream job when a group of elves take him to the North Pole.

- *The Last Chimney of Christmas Eve* by Linda Oatman High (Boyds Mills Press, 2001). Nicholas, an orphan chimney sweep, receives a red coat, a Christmas snow globe, and a simple request from a kind customer to "pass it on." Years later, Nicholas does just that as he dons the coat and visits chimneys everywhere carrying a bag of gifts.

- *The Legend of Old Befana: An Italian Christmas Story* by Tomie dePaola (Harcourt Brace & Company, 1980). Choosing housework over traveling with the three kings to see the newborn king, Befana later packs a basket and sets out to catch up with them. But she never catches the kings or finds the child, and her search continues to this day as she leaves gifts for children every year on January 6, the Feast of the Three Kings.

# Gift-Giver Patterns

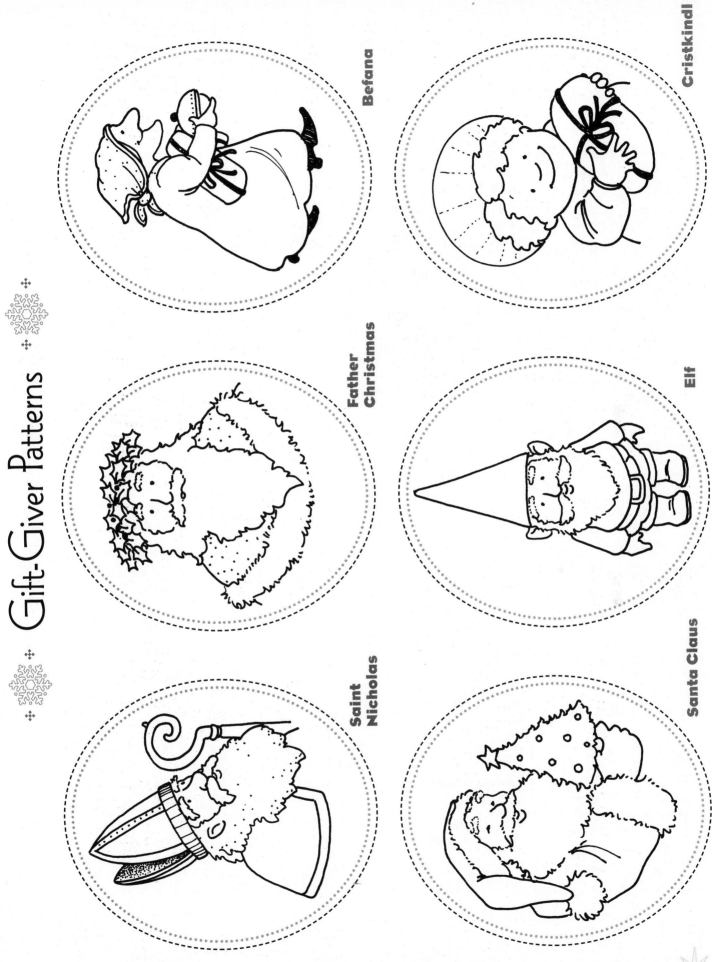

**Befana**

**CristKindl**

**Father Christmas**

**Elf**

**Saint Nicholas**

**Santa Claus**

The Night Before Christmas

ILLUSTRATED BY BRUCE WHATLEY
(HARPERCOLLINS, 1999)

In the stillness of the night, a jolly visitor bounds down the chimney to deliver Christmas surprises for the family, including one special gift for the curious onlooker. Bold, vivid illustrations capture the magic and spirit of Clement C. Moore's classic poem about a visit from St. Nick.

Explain that the author used a number of phrases, such as "nose like a cherry," to help readers imagine St. Nicholas's appearance. Ask children to close their eyes, then reread the description of St. Nick to students. Can they "draw" him in their minds as they listen? Read the text once again, this time writing the descriptive phrases on chart paper. Then invite children to use the descriptions to draw their own versions of St. Nicholas on large sheets of construction paper. When finished, have them label their drawings with phrases from the chart.

## Chimney Surprises (Language Arts)

In this well-loved poem, St. Nick brings a bundle of toys down the chimney. Invite children to pretend to receive surprises from St. Nick with this miniature chimney. To prepare, open both ends of a cracker box and cut off the flaps. Cover the box with red construction paper, then draw bricks so that it resembles a chimney. Then, cut a double flap on one side of the chimney (as shown), fold the flaps back, and cover them with red paper. Draw bricks on the resulting fireplace. Finally, glue magazine cutouts of toys to notecards. To use, invite a child to sit in front of the fireplace. Then drop a card down the chimney. The child removes the card, looks at the picture, and gives clues about the toy's identity to the other children. When a correct guess is made, invite that child to take a turn at the fireplace.

## Christmas Eve Dreams (Language Arts)

On Christmas Eve, sugarplums danced in the children's dreams. In this fun circle game, children recite a list of Christmas items that dance around in their Christmas Eve dreams. First, write on chart paper the Christmas-related items pictured in the book as well as any other items children want to add. To play, the first child recites, "I had a dream on Christmas Eve and in it danced a _____ ," filling in the blank with a word from the list. Each child in turn repeats and adds a word to the sentence, making it one word longer with each turn. The round ends when a child forgets a word or recites the list out of order (you can jingle a bell, if desired). To extend, children can illustrate six to eight dream bubble cutouts with items from the list, then use the cutouts to create a Christmas dream mobile.

## Special "Deer-livery" (Language Arts)

Eight reindeer pulled St. Nick's sleigh to help him deliver toys on Christmas Eve. Invite children to create these reindeer to help deliver their Christmas communications to Santa Claus. To begin, copy and enlarge the reindeer pattern (page 36). Have children cut it out and decorate it, gluing on wiggle eyes, pipe cleaner antlers, a yarn mouth, and any other desired features. Next, they glue a letter-size envelope to the back of their reindeer. Finally, children write their Christmas wish lists or letters to Santa to put in the envelopes. To display, suspend the reindeer from a clothesline. Then, while children are out of the classroom, remove the letters from the envelopes. When they return, encourage them to check to see if the reindeer have delivered their letters yet. Later, secretly send the letters to students' parents (by mail or in an envelope stamped "Confidential") so that "Santa" can respond as parents see fit.

## Related Reading

To help weave the class holiday tapestry, you might have children add:

- a photo or drawing of their homes decorated for Christmas.

- a description of their Christmas Eve activities.

- photos of their Christmas trees and stockings before and after Santa's visit.

- a photo or drawing of their family celebrating Christmas.

- drawings or cards featuring Santa and his reindeer.

- a favorite Christmas ornament, such as a Santa figure, reindeer, gift, or snowflake.

Share these additional classic and enchanted Christmas tales with children:

◆ **The Gift of a Traveler** by Wendy Matthews (Bridgewater Books /Troll, 1996). In this enchanting read-aloud, an old woman recalls for her great-granddaughter how, as a young girl in Romania, she came to receive a special ornament from a mysterious stranger she helped one Christmas Eve.

◆ **How the Grinch Stole Christmas** by Dr. Seuss (Random House, 1985). Planning to put an end to Whoville's Christmas joy, the hard-hearted Grinch dons a Santa disguise and steals all signs of the holiday from the town. In spite of his evildoings, the Whos continue their celebration, and the Grinch realizes that Christmas cannot be stolen from those who carry it in their hearts.

◆ **The Polar Express** by Chris Van Allsburg (Houghton Mifflin Company, 1985). While lying awake on Christmas Eve, a young boy is swept away on a magical train ride to the North Pole, where he receives a special gift from Santa Claus.

◆ **The Twelve Days of Christmas** by Jan Brett (G. P. Putnam's Sons, 1989). In her signature style, Brett brings this familiar Christmas counting song to life with delightfully detailed illustrations and a touch of humor.

◆ **Uncle Vova's Tree** by Patricia Polacco (Philomel Books, 1989). During the first Christmas without beloved Uncle Vova, his family continues the tradition of decorating a tree for the animals and discovers that the magic, wonder, and joy he brought to the holidays does go on.

**reindeer pattern**

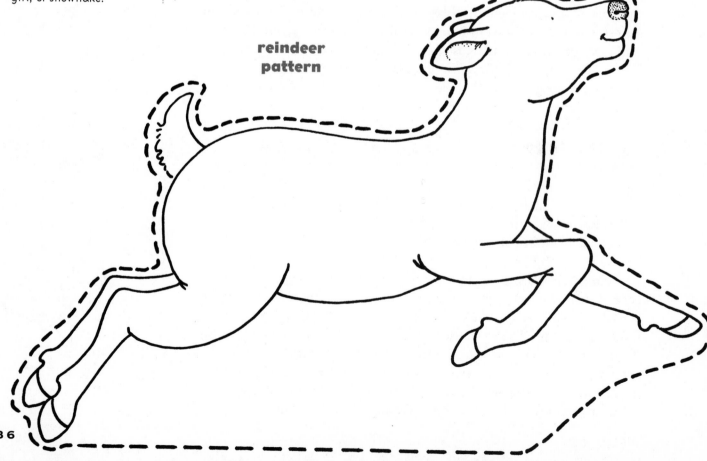

# Seven Candles for Kwanzaa

BY ANDREA DAVIS PINKNEY
(DIAL BOOKS FOR YOUNG
READERS, 1993)

SEVEN CANDLES FOR KWANZAA
*Andrea Davis Pinkney* • *pictures by* *Brian Pinkney*

In the last week of December, a family prepares for and celebrates the seven-day Kwanzaa holiday. During this African-American celebration, family members join together to evaluate their lives, strengthen their commitment to each other and their community, express gratitude for the goodness of life, and honor their ancestors. Each day focuses on a different principle, with the holiday culminating in a feast of traditional foods and a special celebration.

A feast called the *karamu* is the highlight of the last night of Kwanzaa. During the karamu, families honor their ancestors by drinking from the unity cup. Tell children that ancestors are the people, or relatives, who came before them in their families. Invite children to name family members older than themselves— parents, grandparents, aunts, uncles, or even deceased relatives. What makes these people special to children? After sharing, ask children to write about a special family member. Have them illustrate their work, then compile all the pages into a class book dedicated to "those who came before us."

## Holiday Quick Fact

Kwanzaa, an African-American holiday, is celebrated from December 26 to January 1. Dr. Maulana Karenga created the holiday in 1966 to help promote and preserve traditional African values and customs. Although it is not a religious holiday, Kwanzaa is a time for family and friends of African descent to celebrate their heritage, evaluate their lives and community, and make plans for the future.

## Quick-Reference Kinaras (Social Studies and Language Arts)

A candle is lit each day of Kwanzaa to represent the seven principles, called *Nguzo Saba*. Have children follow the directions below to make *kinaras* (candleholders) as reminders of these principles.

**1** Cut out the kinara pattern on page 41.

**2** Fold a 12- by 18-inch sheet of white construction paper in half. Place the pattern on the fold and trace it. Cut out the outline through both layers of paper. When unfolded the cutout will resemble a seven-candle kinara.

**3** Color the kinara and candles, labeling the candles as shown and adding tissue paper flames. For each candle, glue a 2- by 9-inch strip of paper to the base of the kinara.

**4** Use the corresponding candle color to write each day's principle on the front of the adjoining paper strip and its meaning on the back. Accordion-fold the paper strips toward the back of the kinara.

**5** To use, pull out the strips in sequence to name and explain the principle for each day.

## Kinara Colors (Science)

Each candle color in a Kwanzaa kinara has a special meaning: black for the color of the people, red for their struggles, and green for hope. For fun with colors, have children conduct this simple experiment. Cut out three 2- by 6-inch red candles and a 2- by 9-inch black candle. Tape the red and black candles 1/2-inch apart on a neutral wall so that they represent the left side of a kinara. Instruct children to stare at the red candles for 30 seconds and then look at the wall to the right of the black candle. What do they see? Explain that the image of three green candles is an *afterimage* of the red candles— this afterimage color is the complementary color to red. If desired, remove the red candles, tape three green candles to the right of the black candle, and repeat the experiment.

## Cooperative Mural (Social Studies and Art)

Invite children to create a class mural to practice some of the principles of Kwanzaa. First, divide a length of bulletin board paper into seven sections, labeling each section with a Kwanzaa principle. Provide markers, paint, colored chalk, and other drawing tools for student use. Then encourage children to draw pictures under each heading to show what the principle means to them or how they exhibit that principle in their daily activities. As they work, ask students to identify any principles they are practicing at that moment (creativity, cooperation, planning, and so on). Display the completed mural in the hallway for other classes and school visitors to enjoy.

## Reverse Scratchboard Quilt (Art)

The scratchboard art technique used in this story represents creativity, or *kuumba*. Invite children to create their own designs with this reverse scratchboard technique. First, have them tape a 6-inch square of waxed paper to a 6-inch square of red or green construction paper. Then ask students to etch a design on the waxed paper with a toothpick, applying enough pressure to leave an impression of the design on the colored paper. When finished, have them remove the waxed paper and then paint over the colored paper with black watercolor paint. The scratched design will repel the paint, leaving a colored pattern in the black paint. After the paint has dried, display the squares together to create a class Kwanzaa quilt.

## Unique Unity Cups (Language Arts)

Participants in the Kwanzaa celebration drink from a special cup, called the *kikombe cha umoja*, to symbolize togetherness and unity. To make unity cups, have children glue torn tissue paper in Kwanzaa colors around a 15-ounce can, using a paintbrush and water-thinned craft glue. Set the cans aside to dry. (If desired, they can also add decorative patterns with black acrylic paint pens.) To use, give children small Styrofoam cups half-filled with water to set into their unity cups. Signal students to sip their drinks. Then have them remove their drinks and pass their unity cups to others to sip from, using their own personal drinks in the cup. After using the cups as a symbol of class unity, invite children to take them home to use in their own family Kwanzaa celebration, or to offer as *zawadi*, or gifts, to family members.

### Tapestry Tips

To help weave the class holiday tapestry, you might have children add:

- a photo or drawing of a kinara used in their personal Kwanzaa celebrations.

- an mkeka, corn, unity cup, or other item representing a Kwanzaa symbol or principle.

- a photo of their family celebrating Kwanzaa.

- an explanation of the seven Kwanzaa principles.

- a recipe for their favorite holiday food.

## Newspaper Mkekas (Social Studies and Art)

The *mkeka* is a straw place mat that symbolizes the history and tradition of African Americans. To make these unique mkekas, gather newspaper sections with lots of text columns, such as the classifieds or stock market pages. Then cut one 8 1/2- by 11-inch and one 6- by 11-inch sheet of newspaper for each child. Have children paint a red watercolor wash over one sheet and a green wash over the other. To make mkekas, children fold the large sheet of newspaper in half lengthwise. Then, starting at the fold and ending one inch from the opposite edge, they cut slits spaced one inch apart. On the smaller sheet, students cut slits lengthwise from one end of the paper to one inch from the opposite edge, spacing the slits one inch apart. Then they unfold the large paper, carefully weave the strips of the small paper into the slits, as shown, and glue the loose ends in place. Children can insert their mats into clear page protectors and use them as part of a Kwanzaa table setting.

### Related Reading

- ◆ *Celebrating Kwanzaa* by Diane Hoyt-Goldsmith (Holiday House, 1993). This photo-illustrated story follows Andiey and her family as they celebrate Kwanzaa by lighting the kinara and applying the principle for each day of the seven-day holiday.

- ◆ *The Gifts of Kwanzaa* by Synthia Saint James (Albert Whitman & Company, 1994). Written from a child's perspective, simple text explores the origins, symbols, rituals, and principles of Kwanzaa. Swahili words and meanings are laced throughout the story.

- ◆ *The Story of Kwanzaa* by Donna L. Washington (HarperCollins, 1996). African designs border bold illustrations to help convey the origins, history, and customs of Kwanzaa. Explanations of the holiday symbols and seven principles teach readers about the importance of African-American heritage, achievements, and future goals.

# Quick-Reference Kinaras

Place on fold.

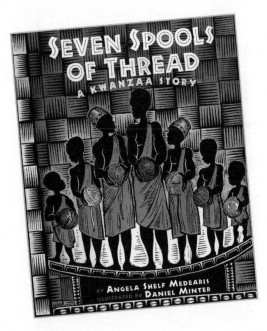

# Seven Spools of Thread: A Kwanzaa Story

BY ANGELA SHELF MEDEARIS
(ALBERT WHITMAN & COMPANY, 2000)

From morning to night, seven Ashanti brothers disagree and argue about anything and everything. On their father's death, though, the brothers discover they must change their ways in order to meet his final request and claim their inheritance. Will they be able to put their differences aside and work together to make gold out of seven spools of thread before sundown? In one intense day, the seven brothers learn the lessons that they failed to grasp all their earlier years—lessons that change the course of their family and community forever.

After reading the story, share with students the African proverb "Sticks in a bundle are unbreakable" (found at the front of the book). Ask them to discuss the meaning of the proverb. Then give a volunteer a single stick and ask him or her to try to break it. What happens? Most likely, the stick breaks easily. Next, give another child a tied bundle of sticks. What happens when the child tries to break the bundle? Use these examples as a springboard to discuss the strength of working together to accomplish goals.

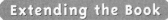
## Practice the Principles (Social Studies and Language Arts)

Help students identify the seven principles of Kwanzaa in the story and in their own activities with this chart. To prepare, label a seven-column chart with the principles. Then write the book title on the left side of the chart. As a class, review the story to find and write examples of each principle. After doing Puzzles and Principles (below), and Colossal Kente Cloths (page 44), add the titles of these activities on the left side of the chart. Then have children write examples of how they practiced each principle in the corresponding column.

| | Umoja (unity) | Kujichagulia (self-determination) | Ujima (collective work) | Ujamaa (cooperative economics) | Nia (purpose) | Kuumba (creativity) | Imani (faith) |
|---|---|---|---|---|---|---|---|
| **Seven Spools of Thread** | shook hands and made peace | took part in solving problem | made loom<br><br>wove cloth together<br><br>worked faster by working together | sold cloth at marketplace | worked to find a way to turn thread to gold | made design in cloth using all colors | had belief in father's decision<br><br>belief in ability to reach goal |

## Puzzles and Principles (Social Studies)

If you're puzzled over how to teach children the value of cooperative work, try this idea. Put the box for a 25-, 50-, or 100-piece puzzle in a center (choose a puzzle suitable for your students' ability level). Then distribute the puzzle pieces evenly among the children. Send several children at a time to the center. Ask them to study the puzzle picture on the box and to try to fit pieces together, using the pieces they brought with them to the center. After a given amount of time, have children leave the center, taking with them any puzzle pieces that they were unable to fit together. Then send another group to the center. Throughout the day, continue to send groups to the center, changing the groupings so that students have the opportunity to work with different classmates (and puzzle pieces). When the puzzle is finally completed, discuss with students the importance of every puzzle piece—and every child's input—in creating a complete picture.

### Holiday Quick Fact

Harambee (hah-rahm-BAY), an African word that means "Let's pull together," is often used during a Kwanzaa celebration.

## Tapestry Tips

To help weave the class holiday tapestry, you might have children add:

- a sample of kente cloth or other fabric with an African design.

- a photo of themselves or their family dressed in traditional African clothing.

- an illustrated poem or story about how the Kwanzaa principles are practiced in their family celebration.

- a map and photos of Africa and its people.

- an illustrated account of a family member, ancestor, or famous African American who has influenced their life.

## Colossal Kente Cloths (Creative Expression and Social Skills)

In the story, the brothers created kente cloth, a traditional fabric of Ghana. Divide the class into groups of up to seven, then invite students to create patterned kente cloths with this activity. To begin, give each group three to seven colors of crepe paper streamers, each about four feet long (to represent thread), scissors, and a length of bulletin board paper. Then challenge children in each group to work together to weave a large patterned cloth with their threads. When they complete their cloths, have groups glue the thread ends to the background paper. Then display the creative kente cloths for all to enjoy.

## A Cooperative Community (Social Studies)

The fourth Kwanzaa principle, *ujamaa*, encourages people to support each other in business. Have children create this community web to develop an understanding of how businesses can contribute to each other's success. First, work with children to create a list of businesses in your community. Then write the name of ten businesses, each on a separate half-sheet of paper. Arrange the papers in a circular pattern on a bulletin board or wall space within easy reach of students. To use, give one child at a time yarn, scissors, and tape. Using the businesses on the display, have the child describe a way in which one business can support another. Then ask the child to tape a length of yarn between the two businesses. As children work, point out how businesses can both support and be supported by many other businesses. To extend, invite students to set up a mini-community in your classroom. Then have them role-play ways in which businesses and residents can support one another.

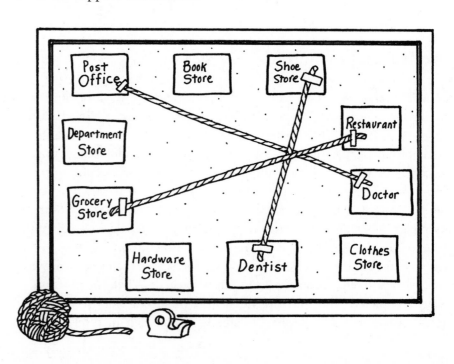

## Spinning for Sevens (Math)

Seven brothers. Seven spools. Seven baskets. Use this small-group game to reinforce basic addition and multiplication facts for the "seven" family.

**1** Color and cut out the patterns on page 46.

**2** Glue the circle onto a paper plate.

**3** Use a marker to trace the arrow onto a margarine or yogurt container lid and cut it out. Use a permanent marker to write the number "7" on the tip of the arrow and punch a hole in the other end, as indicated. To make the spinner, attach the arrow to the paper plate with a paper fastener, as shown. Check that it spins freely.

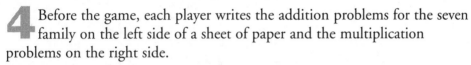

**4** Before the game, each player writes the addition problems for the seven family on the left side of a sheet of paper and the multiplication problems on the right side.

**5** To play, each player in turn flips a penny to determine which operation to use: heads for addition and tails for multiplication. Then the player spins the arrow. According to how the penny lands, the child adds or multiplies the 7 on the arrow and the number it points to, then writes the answer by the corresponding problem on his or her paper.

◎ If a player spins a problem that has already been answered on his or her paper, play moves to the next person.

◎ If the arrow lands on the 7, the player gets another turn (even if that problem has already been correctly completed).

The game ends when all players have filled in the answers to their problems. Have players use a set of "seven" fact cards to check their answers.

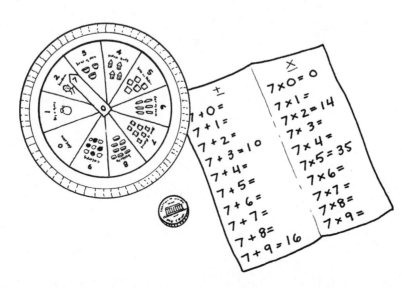

*Related Reading*

◆ **Habari Gani? What's the News?: A Kwanzaa Story** by Sundaira Morninghouse (Open Hand Publishing, 1992). Kia enjoys preparing for Kwanzaa and participating in family and community activities during the week-long holiday. Swahili words for the holiday's symbols, principles, and concepts are cleverly woven into the story to help explain and emphasize their importance.

◆ **Imani's Gift at Kwanzaa** by Denise Burden-Patmon (Simon & Schuster Books for Young Readers, 1992). During her family's Kwanzaa celebration, Imani learns about her African heritage, cultural values, and the importance of unity among people.

◆ **A Kwanzaa Miracle** by Sharon Shavers Gayle (Troll Communications, 1996). A broken window gives Ashley and Darryl a chance to meet their mean neighbor, Mrs. Jackson. Realizing that she's just lonely, the children make plans to honor Mrs. Jackson, along with a surprise guest, at their community Kwanzaa celebration.

# Spinning for Sevens

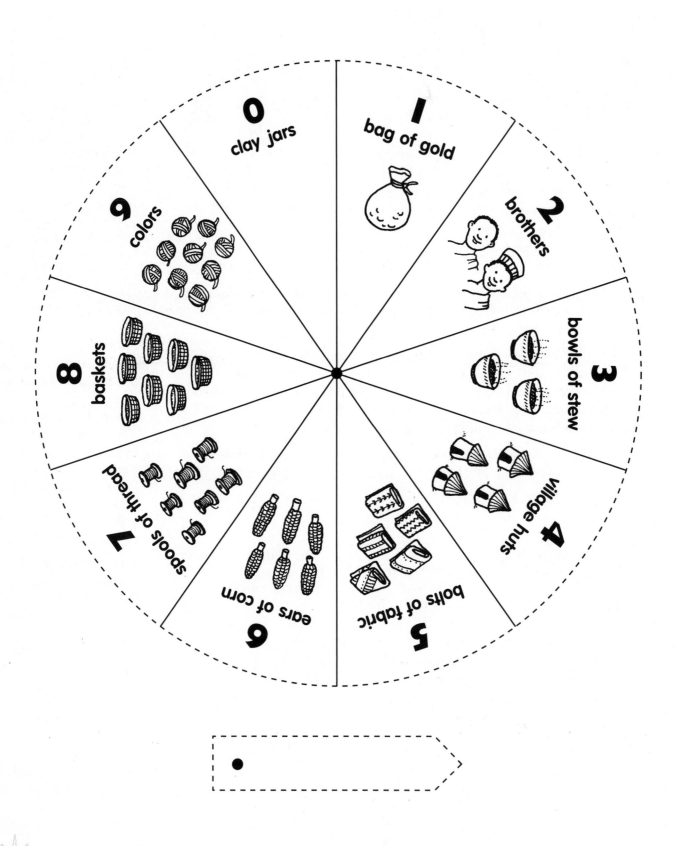

Teaching About Winter Holidays With Favorite Picture Books    Scholastic Teaching Resources

# K Is for Kwanzaa: A Kwanzaa Alphabet Book

BY JUWANDA G. FORD

(SCHOLASTIC, 1997)

From *Africa*, *bendera*, and *candle* to *xylophone*, *yams*, and *zawadi*, this book is filled with symbols, facts, and pictures related to Kwanzaa, the African-American holiday. Readers will learn the ABCs of the celebration along with information about African culture, history, and customs.

Alphabetically list the words from the book on a sheet of chart paper. Review the words and their meanings with students. Then invite children to add other Kwanzaa-related words beside the listed words that begin with the same letter. After completing the list, remind children that storytelling is a popular tradition among African cultures. Ask them to think of ways in which they might use words from the list in a story. Afterward, have individuals or small groups write and illustrate special Kwanzaa stories to share with the class. Alternatively, children might record their stories on a tape recorder or create puppets and props to use in telling their stories.

## Holiday Quick Fact

Africa, the second largest continent on earth, is also the second most populated continent. It is home to the world's largest desert (the Sahara) and the world's longest river (the Nile).

## Corn for the Kids (Social Studies and Language Arts)

*Muhindi* (also called *vibunzi*) are ears of corn that are placed on the mkeka. Each ear of corn represents a child in the family. Invite children to create muhindi to represent themselves in their class family. First, ask them to color and cut out the corn and husk patterns on page 50. Then have them put the pieces together with a paper fastener, as shown, to make an ear of corn. To complete, have children write their name on the left husk, draw a self-portrait on the right husk, and write descriptive words about themselves on the corn. Display the muhindi on a bulletin board backed with a tablecloth or patterned wrapping paper that resembles a woven mat. Make sure the husks are left free to be opened and closed. Then invite children to share their muhindi with the class.

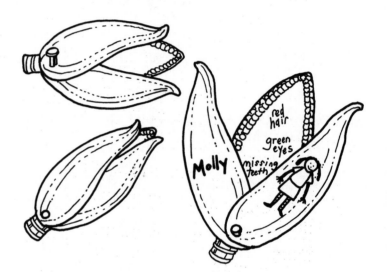

## Zawadi With Zest (Creative Expression and Art)

Ask children to list things mentioned in the book that can be made into *zawadi* (gifts) or that can be used to make zawadi. They might also add their own suggestions to the list. Display the list as a reference. Then provide students with various craft materials, including as many as possible from the list (such as fabric scraps, corn husks, and raffia). Encourage children to tap into their *kuumba*, or creativity, to make a gift for someone special. After children have completed their gifts, have them tell the class about what they made and how. Then invite students to take home their zawadi to present to their special person.

## Dashing Dashikis (Art)

*Dashikis* are simple African shirts that are worn by males and females. Invite students to decorate personalized dashikis to wear during your classroom Kwanzaa activities.

BACK                    FRONT

◎ To begin, help them cut the neck and arms from a large brown paper bag, as shown. (Children can leave the side flaps attached to use as sleeves or cut them off for a sleeveless dashiki.)

◎ Then have them use markers, crayons, and glitter pens to decorate their dashikis in colorful patterns.

◎ Alternatively, children can stamp designs on their shirts using paint and sponge or vegetable shapes.

*Related Reading*

◆ **Kwanzaa Kids** by Joan Holub (Penguin Puffin Books for Young Readers, 2002). Simple, rhyming text describes the fun ways in which a group of children celebrate the meaning and traditions of Kwanzaa, from lighting the kinara and making gifts to playing games and enjoying a holiday feast.

◆ **My First Kwanzaa Book** by Deborah M. Newton Chocolate (Scholastic, 1992). It's Kwanzaa time, a time for this young boy's family to gather and celebrate its heritage with African clothing, flags, stories, music, crafts, and foods. Each two-page spread features a Kwanzaa date, the corresponding principle, and a lighted kinara for the day.

*Tapestry Tips*

To help weave the class holiday tapestry, you might have children add:

● a calendar showing the dates of Kwanzaa.

● photos or samples of handmade gifts, or zawadi.

● an item representing a special holiday tradition, such as a photo of a family quilt, or a miniature version of the kinara.

● a holiday card, candle, or sample of gift wrap representing Kwanzaa.

● illustrated word cards for numbers and objects, written in Swahili and English.

# Corn for the Kids

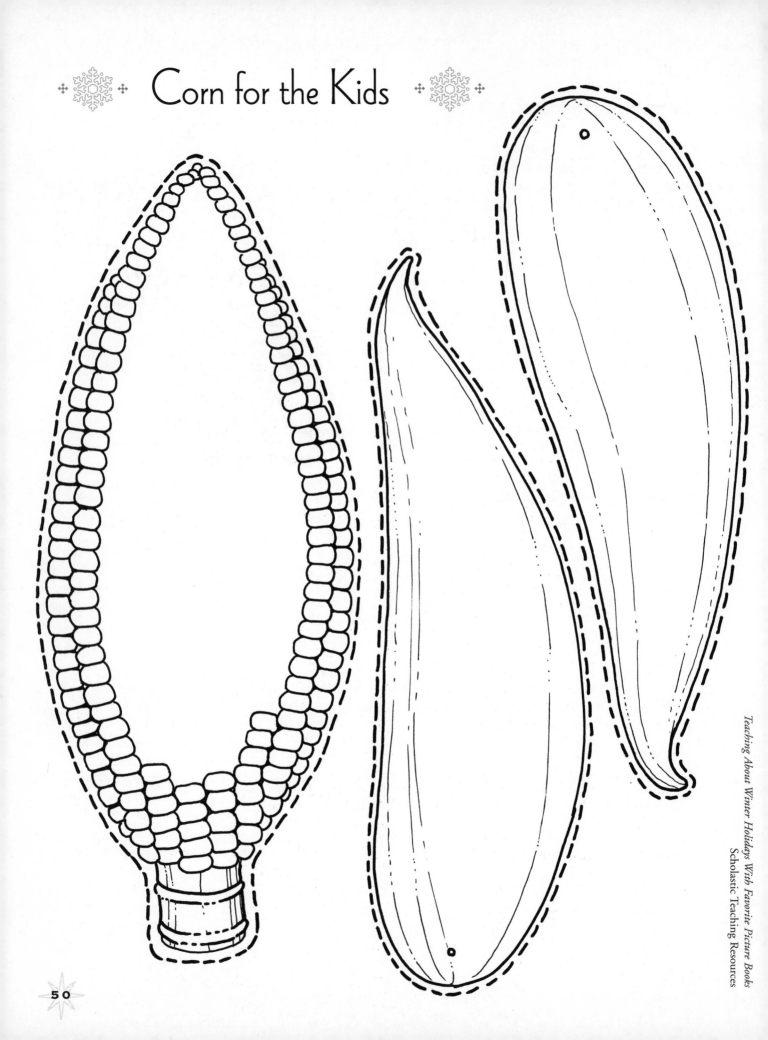

# Lion Dancer: Ernie Wan's Chinese New Year

BY KATE WATERS
(SCHOLASTIC, 1990)

**F**ollow Ernie Wan as he prepares for the most important day of his life—performing the Lion Dance in the Chinatown parade. As part of the preparations for the Chinese New Year event, Ernie and his family follow the many customs of their people, from cooking and eating traditional foods to wearing new clothes to giving children red envelopes with money. On parade day, Ernie keeps his lion in constant motion as the activity around him increases and the noise intensifies. Finally, the parade reaches his neighborhood—and it's his turn to perform a Lion Dance that will bring honor to his family.

Ernie spent time practicing his dance so that he could perform it in the parade with as few mistakes as possible. Ask children to share their thoughts on the importance of practicing for occasions such as performing a dance, participating in a sports event, or singing a song. Is practice equally important for activities such as writing and solving math problems? Invite students to tell about some activities they had to practice before they were able to do them well (riding a bike, writing their names, tying shoes, and so on).

# Paper Bag Lions (Art and Movement)

The Chinese believe that the Lion Dance chases away harm and brings good luck to homes and businesses. Invite children to create personal lion puppets from large brown paper bags.

**1** To begin, they cut out a panel from the bag, as shown.

**2** Then they cut out a 4- by 6-inch window from the bottom of the bag.

**3** To lengthen the puppet, students glue the removed panel to the end of the bag.

**4** Next, they paint a bold pattern on the bag in bright colors, such as red and yellow.

**5** To make eyes, they cut a paper plate in half and paint each half to resemble an eye. If desired, they can use gold foil circles for the pupils.

**6** Then children glue the eyes onto the puppet and add other features such as feather lashes, crepe paper nostrils, and construction paper ears and tongue.

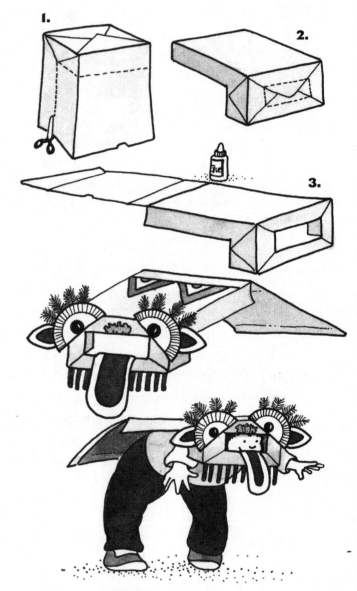

To use, children put their heads into the puppets so that they can see out the window. Then they dance and move to a selection of lively music. As an alternative, you might have children make smaller hand puppets from paper lunch bags. For these, children simply cut out the panel, glue it to the end of the bag, and decorate the lion with paint and craft materials.

## New Year's Banners

(Language Arts and Art)

The children go to a special school to learn how to write in Chinese. During the holiday, families display red banners with two-line Chinese New Year messages written on them. Ask students to make up messages to express good wishes for the new year, such as, "May you make good grades and have lots of fun." To make banners, have children glue a 12-inch sentence strip to the top and bottom edge of a 12- by 18-inch sheet of red (or gold) foil gift wrap. Then have them write their messages on the paper with a black permanent marker. Students can use carrot sticks (cut in half lengthwise) and a contrasting paint color—such as black—to stamp a simple geometric pattern around the border of their banners. When completed, help children add a yarn hanger to their banners.

## Lucky Money Math (Math)

On Chinese New Year, children and unmarried adults receive *lai-see*, red envelopes that carry good luck messages and contain money. Use these simple "lucky money" envelopes to give children practice in money skills. To make envelopes, cut 4-inch squares from red paper. With one corner of the square pointing away from you, write a money amount in the center of each square. Then fold the corners of the square toward the center, as shown, and seal each "envelope" with a gold reusable seal. Put the envelopes in a basket in your math center, along with pencil and paper. To use, children draw two envelopes from the basket, open them, and write addition equations with the money values. They solve the problems, and then have classmates check their work for correctness. When finished, children reseal the envelopes and return them to the basket.

## Fresh-Start Firecrackers (Language Arts)

According to Chinese tradition, the loud explosion of firecrackers frightens away evil spirits. Invite children to make these firecrackers to scare away bad habits and behaviors. First, children glue red tissue paper over one end of a toilet paper tube. Then, on a few slips of paper, they write positive behaviors they want to display in the new year. They put the paper slips in the tube and cover the open end with tissue paper. Then students glue a piece of red construction paper around their tube, trimming the excess paper as needed, and write their name on their tube. Finally, they add a thin paper fuse to one end of the firecracker. To make a string of firecrackers, tie red yarn around each firecracker, then use clothespins to attach them to a length of red ribbon. On Chinese New Year, invite children to remove their firecrackers, "pop" open one end to scare away their bad habits and behaviors, and remove the papers from inside. Ask them to read their papers as reminders of the behaviors they want to display in order to have a fresh start for the new year.

## Related Reading

◆ **The Runaway Rice Cake** by Ying Chang Compestine (Simon & Schuster Books for Young Readers, 2001). The Changs chase a runaway new year's rice cake through the village until it collides with a hungry old woman. With nothing left for their own feast, the family shares the rice cake with the woman. Returning home, the Changs find that their kindness is rewarded with an abundance of friends...and food!

◆ **Sam and the Lucky Money** by Karen Chinn (Lee & Low Books, 1995). While shopping to spend his new year's money, Sam accidentally steps on a homeless man's bare foot. Later, undecided about what to buy, Sam is moved to return to the less fortunate man and offer the lucky money to him.

◆ **This Next New Year** by Janet S. Wong (Frances Foster Books, 2000). A young Chinese-Korean boy anticipates getting a fresh start for the new year as he grooms himself, scrubs the house, resolves to be positive and brave, and focuses on making his dreams come true.

### Tapestry Tips

To help weave the class holiday tapestry, you might have children add:

● a photo of their participation in a Chinese New Year parade and/or celebration.

● an illustrated poem or story about their favorite Chinese New Year traditions.

● samples of lai-see, Chinese writing symbols, noisemakers, plastic models of firecrackers, and other items related to Chinese New Year.

● a recipe for a favorite Chinese New Year food.

● a photo, drawing, or miniature model of a Chinese New Year dragon or lion.

● a map and photos of China and its people.

# Happy New Year, Everywhere!

BY ARLENE ERLBACH
(THE MILLBROOK PRESS, 2000)

How do the Greeks, Japanese, or Indian people celebrate the new year? Discover how—and when—people from these and many other countries across the globe celebrate the new year. Filled with engaging text and illustrations, this book features the unique new year customs of 20 different countries. Each country is shown on a world map, along with the name of its new year's celebration, the new year's greeting in the country's official language, one or more typical celebration customs, and a bonus hands-on activity to help readers experience an aspect of the country's culture.

Write the name of each featured country on a slip of paper, fold the slips, and put them in a basket. After sharing the book, ask children to draw country names from the basket. Then invite children to take turns locating their country on a globe or large world map. On what continent is their country found? Ask them to recall information about the country's new year's celebrations. Then revisit the spread in the book to refresh or expand students' recollections. To extend, have children research their country to learn more about its population, resources, and culture. Invite them to share their findings with the class.

## Cross-Cultural Celebrations (Social Studies and Language Arts)

Which new year's customs from the book appeal to students? Why? Are these customs they might like to include in their own celebrations? Discuss, and then have children create posters to show their ideal new year's celebrations. On large sheets of construction paper, have them draw decorations, food, costumes, noisemakers, and so on, that they would enjoy for their own celebrations. These can be customs of other countries found in the book or those of their own creation. As they work, have students write the country of influence beneath the corresponding drawing. To complete their posters, invite them to glue confetti and crinkle strips around the edges to create a festive border. After children share with the class, encourage them to take home their celebration posters and include some of the ideas in their family new year's celebrations.

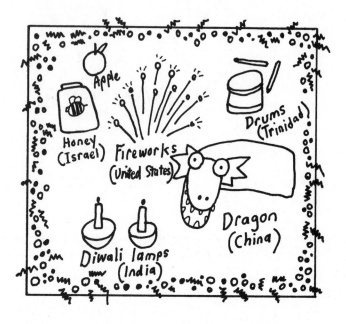

## New Year's Calendar (Social Studies)

Not every country celebrates New Year's Day on January 1. To help children compare the dates of new year's celebrations in different countries, divide a chart into 12 columns. Then write a different month at the top of each column. Have students refer to the book and then write the name of each country under the month in which it celebrates the new year. Beside the country, write the number of days spent in celebration. To extend, ask children to research other countries to learn when they observe the new year. Add these countries to the chart. Use the chart results to determine which months are most and least popular for new year's celebrations, as well as which country holds the longest celebration.

# New Year's Greetings Wig (Social Studies)

Invite children to create these fun wigs to help them express new year's greetings in the language of other countries.

**1** To begin, children staple the ends of a sentence strip together to make a fitted headband.

**2** Next, they cut six 2 1/2- by 12-inch strips of construction paper (any color).

**3** They then write a country name (from the book) on the end of each strip and the country's new year's greeting and its meaning along the length of the strip, as shown.

**4** Students glue each strip to the headband to create hair, leaving a wide gap between two strips.

**5** Then they tightly wrap each strip, or hair, around a pencil and release it to create a curl.

Invite children to wear their wigs during your class new year's celebration. When they want to wish a classmate "Happy New Year" in another country's language, students simply name the country. Then the classmate straightens the corresponding curl on the well-wisher's wig to read the greeting.

## Tapestry Tips

To help weave the class holiday tapestry, you might have children add:

- a photo of their personal or cultural new year's celebrations.

- an illustrated poem or story about their favorite new year's traditions.

- a favorite noisemaker, party favor, decoration, or holiday card used to celebrate the new year.

- a description of ways they include traditions from other countries in their personal new year's celebrations.

- an explanation of the customs and symbols of their culture's new year's celebrations.

- maps of countries represented in their new year's celebrations.

- an illustrated list of their new year's resolutions.

## Holiday Hand Puppets (Social Studies)

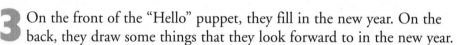

Children can wave out the old year and welcome in the new year with these "hand-y" holiday puppets.

**1** Copy page 59 onto heavyweight paper for each student. Students then color and cut out the patterns.

**2** On the front of the "Goodbye" puppet, students write the year that just ended. Then, on the back, they draw a few things they enjoyed in the old year.

**3** On the front of the "Hello" puppet, they fill in the new year. On the back, they draw some things that they look forward to in the new year.

**4** Next, students glue a wide craft stick to the back of each puppet, in the center.

**5** To complete their puppets, students stack them back to back and twist half of a pipe cleaner around the sticks to hold them together.

To share with others, children separate the puppets, read the poems, and show the pictures on the back of each.

### Related Reading

◆ *Dumpling Soup* by Jama Kim Rattigan (Little, Brown and Company, 1993). When Marisa helps make the dumplings for her family's traditional new year's meal, she worries that they won't taste good enough. Set in Hawaii, this story about a multicultural family weaves Hawaiian, Japanese, English, and Korean words throughout the text.

◆ *First Night* by Harriet Ziefert (G. P. Putnam's Sons, 1999). With Amanda Dade in the lead, the First Night parade is a sight indeed! Cumulative verse builds a cast of fun, colorful characters to usher in the new year.

◆ *New Year's Day: A True Book* by Dana Meachen Rau (Children's Press, 2000). From staying up late to welcoming the new year, this photo-illustrated book provides interesting, factual information on the history and traditions of new year's celebrations in the United States and around the world.

◆ *P. Bear's New Year's Party* by Paul Owen Lewis (Tricycle Press, 1989). P. Bear invites his best-dressed friends to join him for a special new year's celebration. Counting and time-telling skills are reinforced with red numbers, number words, and clock times set in a black-and-white color scheme.

---

## Holiday Quick Facts

Some believe that the idea of Father Time came from the mythical Greek god Kronos, who reminded the people that all things come to an end. Another Greek myth, in which the god Dionysus died every winter and was reborn each spring, is believed to have inspired the idea of Baby New Year.

# Holiday Hand Puppets

Hello, _____
You'll be lots of fun.
The first day is here now.
The new year has begun!

Name _____

Goodbye, _____
You've been lots of fun.
The last day is here now.
The old year is done!

Name _____

# Creative Winter Holiday Crafts

Celebrate diversity with this collection of simple ideas for gifts, decorations, and party favors designed for any winter holiday celebration. For each of these crafts, children have the flexibility to shape the project to fit the specific holidays they observe. Guide them in following the directions for any of the projects on pages 60–62. Then all they have to do is select the colors and symbols related to their holiday choices, and start creating!

## Materials

* paper plate
* crayons
* scissors
* samples of gift wrap decorated with holiday symbols
* greeting cards with pictures of holiday symbols
* six 20-inch lengths of crepe paper streamers (in holiday colors)
* glue
* stapler
* 2-foot length of yarn
* two 3- by 7-inch strips of construction paper

## Symbol Mobiles

Children can display the symbols and colors of their favorite holidays with these unique mobiles.

1 Color both sides of the paper plate with a color to represent the selected holiday.

2 Cut out holiday symbols from the gift wrap and greeting cards (or draw and cut out symbols). Glue the symbols to the crepe paper streamers.

3 Staple each streamer to the plate, as shown.

4 Poke two holes near the center of the plate. Thread the yarn through the holes and tie the ends together to create a hanger.

5 Write a holiday message on both strips of construction paper. Glue the back of the strips together with the yarn hanger between them, as shown.

## Holiday Play-Clay Lights

Invite children to shape holiday candleholders, candles, and firecrackers from this easy play dough recipe. Mix all the ingredients together, adding small amounts of flour or water until firm. After mixing the clay, students can form it into the desired shapes, adding details such as candle flames and firecracker fuses. Have them set aside the clay shapes to dry for several days and then paint the projects in holiday colors.

### Play-Clay Recipe

(makes enough clay for 10 children)

☆ 2 1/2 cups flour

☆ 1 cup salt

☆ 3/4 teaspoon alum
(available at pharmacies)

☆ 1 cup water

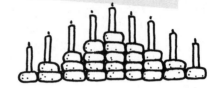

## Giant Candles and "Crackers"

Recycle plastic soda bottles and chip canisters for these holiday favors that carry special greetings. Encourage children to present their candles or firecrackers as gifts to family or friends.

**1** For a candle, remove the lid from the plastic soda bottle. For a firecracker, cut a one-inch hole in the center of the chip canister lid. Snap the lid onto the canister.

**2** Coat the bottle or canister with glue. Then completely cover the container with torn paper (leave the top opening in the bottle and chip canister uncovered).

**3** Apply another coat of glue over the paper. Glue on additional layers of paper as desired. Then allow the glue to dry thoroughly.

**4** For each holiday favor, write a holiday message on a paper strip. Glue one end of the strip to a craft stick, as shown. Wrap the paper around the stick and secure it with a paper clip.

**5** For the candle, glue a paper "flame" to the other end of the craft stick and insert it into the bottle with the flame end sticking out. For the firecracker, insert the craft stick "fuse" into the chip canister firecracker.

**6** To use, remove the flame or the fuse and unwrap the paper to read the holiday message.

### Materials

* tapered plastic soda bottle (for candle) or short chip canister (for firecracker)
* torn tissue paper in holiday colors (or torn holiday gift wrap)
* water-thinned craft glue
* paintbrush
* wide craft stick
* 3- by 5-inch paper strip
* tape
* paper clip

## Materials

..........✦..........

* ★ card pattern,
  page 63
* ★ crayons
* ★ scissors

## Festive Family Cards

Family gatherings are the feature of these unusual holiday cards. Invite children to use their cards to tell others about their family winter celebrations.

**1** In the spaces on your card, draw a picture of each person who comes to your family's holiday gathering. If more space is needed, use an additional copy of the card.

**2** Cut out the pattern. If more than one pattern is used, glue the copies together to make one long card.

**3** Write each person's name on the back of his or her picture.

**4** On the table, draw and label foods that are enjoyed during your family holiday gathering. Or, draw a picture of something that symbolizes the gathering, such as gifts for a gift exchange.

**5** Fold the card as shown. Write a holiday message on the card. Then draw a colorful border around the edges.

## Beautiful Banners

Deck the halls with festive banners! Let children take home these beautiful banners to use as decorations for their holiday celebrations.

**1** Use fabric pens to write a holiday message on the felt or fabric square.

**2** Glue on glitter, confetti shapes, tinsel, and other craft items to create a decorative border.

**3** Staple the square to the cut paper towel tube, as shown.

**4** Punch two holes in the tube. Then lace a ribbon through the holes and tie the ends in a bow.

## Materials

..........✦..........

* ★ 12-inch square solid felt or fabric (in a holiday color)
* ★ fabric pens in contrasting holiday colors
* ★ craft glue
* ★ glitter, holiday confetti shapes, tinsel, and other holiday craft items
* ★ paper towel tube cut in half lengthwise
* ★ hole punch
* ★ thin ribbon

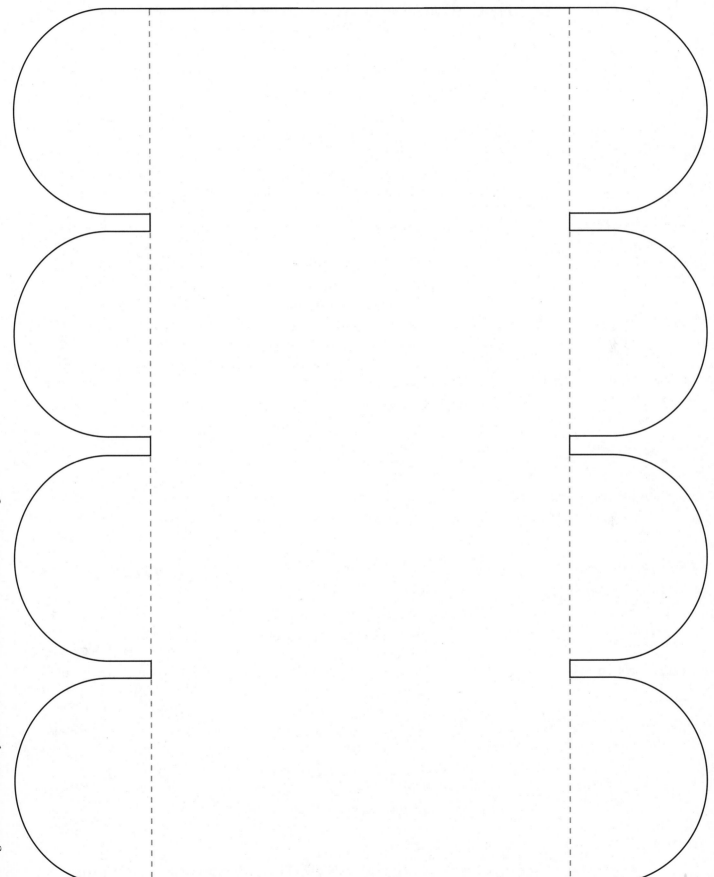

# Winter Holiday Resources  *U*se the following resources for holiday-related history, stories, games, and other activities.

## GENERAL

### Books

*Children Just Like Me: Celebrations* by Anabel Kindersley (Dorling Kindersley, 1997).

### Web Sites

www.billybear4kids.com/holidays/fun.htm
http://theholidayspot.com
www.historychannel.com/exhibits/holidays

## HANUKKAH

### Books

*A Hanukkah Treasury* by Eric Kimmel (Henry Holt, 1998).

*A World of Holidays: Hanukkah* by Ann Clark, David Rose, and Gill Rose (Steck-Vaughn, 1998).

*Hanukkah: Celebrating the Holiday of Lights* by Arlene Erlbach (Enslow Publishers, 2002).

### Web Sites

www.night.net/kids/hanukkah.html-ssi
www.torahtots.com/holidays/chanuka/chanuk.htm

## LAS POSADAS

### Books

*Las Posadas: An Hispanic Christmas Celebration* by Diane Hoyt-Goldsmith (Holiday House, 1999).

### Web Sites

www.theholidayspot.com/christmas/worldxmas/mexico.htm
www.kidsdomain.com/holiday/xmas/around/mexico.html
www.californiamall.com/holiday traditions/traditions-mexico.htm

## CHRISTMAS

### Books

*Christmas Around the World* by Mary D. Lankford (Morrow Junior Books, 1995).

*Christmas* by Alice K. Flanagan (Compass Point Books, 2002).

*Christmas: Celebrating Life, Giving, and Kindness* by Arlene Erlbach (Enslow Publishers, 2001).

### Web Sites

www.northpole.net
http://www.christmas.com/worldview

## KWANZAA

### Books

*The Children's Book of Kwanzaa: A Guide to Celebrating the Holiday* by Dolores Johnson (Atheneum Books for Young Readers, 1996).

*The Seven Days of Kwanzaa* by Angela Shelf Medearis (Scholastic, 1994).

*Kwanzaa Karamu: Cooking and Crafts for a Kwanzaa Feast* by April A. Brady (Carolrhoda Books, 1995).

### Web Sites

www.globalindex.com/kwanzaa
www.factmonster.com/spot/kwanzaa1.html

## CHINESE NEW YEAR

### Books

*Chinese New Year: A Time for Parades, Family, and Friends* by Fay Robinson (Enslow Publishers, 2001).

*Celebrating Chinese New Year* by Diane Hoyt-Goldsmith (Holiday House, 1998).

*Chinese New Year* by Dianne M. Macmillan (Enslow Publishers, 1994).

### Web Sites

www.c-c-c.org/chineseculture/festival/newyear/newyear.html
www.kiddyhouse.com/CNY
www.educ.uvic.ca/faculty/mroth/438/CHINA/chinese_new_year.html

## NEW YEAR'S DAY

### Books

*Happy New Year* by Emily Kelley (Carolrhoda Books, 1984).

*We Celebrate New Year* by Bobbie Kalman (Crabtree Publishing Company, 1985).

*Happy New Year!* by Emery Bernhard (Lodestar Books, 1996).

### Web Site

http://wilstar.com/holidays/newyear.htm

---

Please note that when this book went to press, the Web sites listed here were current and the material on them was appropriate for children's use. However, because Web-site content is subject to change, it's a good idea to preview each site before sending children to the computer.